TWO VIEWS OF MAIN STREET, COLUMBIA
LOOKING NORTH FROM THE STATE HOUSE

AS SHERMAN LEFT IT IN FEBRUARY, 1865

As it is To-day, December 14, 1926

OUSTING
THE CARPETBAGGER
FROM
SOUTH CAROLINA

By

HENRY T. THOMPSON

NEGRO UNIVERSITIES PRESS
NEW YORK

Originally published in 1926
by the R. L. Bryan Company

Reprinted from a copy in the collections
of the Brooklyn Public Library

Reprinted 1969 by
Negro Universities Press
A DIVISION OF GREENWOOD PRESS, INC.
NEW YORK

SBN 8371-2706-8

PRINTED IN UNITED STATES OF AMERICA

DEDICATED TO

THE RED SHIRTS

OF 1876,

IN EVERY WALK OF LIFE, TO WHOSE UNCEASING VIGILANCE, TIRELESS ENERGY

AND EXALTED PATRIOTISM, WAS DUE THE OVERTHROW

OF REPUBLICAN MISRULE AND THE OUSTING

OF THE CARPETBAGGER FROM

SOUTH CAROLINA

Semicentennial of Hampton's Inauguration

A JOINT RESOLUTION to Declare December 14, 1926, a Legal Holiday, to provide for the Proper Observance Thereof, and to Make an Appropriation to Defray the Expenses Incident to said Observance.

Whereas, December 14, 1926, is the Fiftieth Anniversary of the Inauguration of General Wade Hampton as Governor of the State of South Carolina; and

Whereas, This is a momentous event in the history of the State, this day marking the anniversary of the culmination of a patriotic and self-sacrificing effort on the part of our citizens for the overthrow of the Radical Rule which had destroyed the property and threatened the civilization of the State; and

Whereas, It is well to recall to the minds of our people this crisis in our history and to remind them that the questions and issues decided by the election of General Hampton were not only State-wide, but Nation-wide in their effect; and

Whereas, It is further desirous that as far as possible there be a recognition of those who bore an active part in the "Red Shirt Campaign" under the leadership of General Hampton and his able lieutenants and co-workers; now, therefore,

Section 1. *December 14th, a Legal Holiday in 1926.*—Be it resolved by the General Assembly of the State of South Carolina: That December 14th be, and the same is hereby, declared a Legal Holiday, for the year 1926 only.

Section 2. *Celebration.*—That a Committee composed of one man and one woman from each Congressional District in the State be appointed by the Governor to arrange for a proper observance and celebration of this day at the Capitol at Columbia, South Carolina, with full power and authority to arrange a program in keeping with and responsive to this celebration.

Section 3. *Appropriation.*—That a sum not exceeding Five Thousand ($5,000.00) Dollars be appropriated for the purpose of defraying the necessary expenses of the observance and celebration of this day.

Section 4. This Resolution shall take effect immediately upon its approval by the Governor.

Approved the 23rd day of March, A. D. 1926.

(Note: The idea of the Hampton Semicentennial originated with W. P. Houseal, of Columbia.)

iv

CONTENTS

v

FOREWORD

Within the limits of a volume of this size, that endeavors to set forth all happenings of importance during a period of twelve years, when history in South Carolina was being written daily, almost hourly, it is manifestly impossible to mention by name the leaders in every county in 1876, numbering, in all, more than a hundred, who rendered incalculable service in the redemption of the State. Only the names are mentioned, therefore, which are necessary for following the thread of the narrative.

Three men stood out conspicuously as next to Hampton in what was achieved in redeeming the State—M. C. Butler, M. W. Gary, and A. C. Haskell.

Matthew Calbraith Butler, of Edgefield County, was born near Greenville, S. C., in 1836. He entered the South Carolina College in 1854, but left without graduating in 1857. He was admitted to the bar in that year, and was elected to the Legislature in 1860. Entering the Confederate service as a Captain in the Hampton Legion, he became a Major-General. A wound received at Brandy Station cost him the loss of a leg. In 1866, General Butler was again elected to the Legislature, and in 1877 he was elected to the United States Senate, continuing a member of that body for three terms. In the Spanish-American War he served as a Major-General of Volunteers in the United States army, and as a member of the commission to receive the island of Cuba from Spain. He died in 1909.

Martin Witherspoon Gary, of Edgefield County, was born at Cokesbury, in Abbeville County, in 1831. He graduated from Harvard in 1854, and was admitted to the bar in 1855. At the outbreak of the War of Secession, he entered the Confederate army as a Captain in the Hampton Legion. He was frequently promoted, and just before the war ended, was appointed a Major-General. General Gary was elected State Senator from Edgefield County in 1876. Though refused a seat in that body by the Republican majority, he acted, as did the other Democratic Senators, with the Wallace House. He served the term of four years in the Senate, and then declined

vii

a re-election. General Gary, besides being an accomplished lawyer, was a successful farmer, and he amassed a considerable fortune. He died in 1881.

Alexander Cheves Haskell, of Richland County, was born in Abbeville County in 1839. He graduated from the South Carolina College in 1860. He enlisted in the Confederate army as a private and rose to the rank of Colonel. He was twice severely wounded. Colonel Haskell was admitted to the bar in 1865, and was in the same year elected to the Legislature. In 1867 he was made professor of law in the University of South Carolina. In the campaign of 1876 he was chairman of the State Democratic Executive Committee. Colonel Haskell was elected Associate Justice of the State Supreme Court in 1877, to succeed the negro Wright, but resigned in 1879 to become president of the Charlotte, Columbia & Augusta Railroad. This position he held until 1888, when he became president of a Columbia bank. Colonel Haskell died in 1910.

ESPECIAL ACKNOWLEDGMENT TO JOHN S. REYNOLDS

The author has endeavored to acknowledge, at proper places in the text, his obligation to others in the preparation of this book. Especial acknowledgment is due, however, to John S. Reynolds' work, Reconstruction in South Carolina, for the great aid that it gave him. Mr. Reynolds has furnished to the student of the Reconstruction period in South Carolina a veritable storehouse of valuable information, which will increase in value every year.

CHAPTER I

Centennial of the Battle of Fort Moultrie—1876

The hottest day in the South within the memory of the proverbial oldest inhabitant was June 28, 1876. In the ancient and historic city of Charleston, South Carolina, which rested "in the strong arms of its palm-crowned isles," the sweltering rays of a scorching summer sun struck with its intense heat the long line of a civil and military parade staged in celebration of the Centennial of the Battle of Fort Moultrie—the first great effort in South Carolina to throw off the galling British yoke. The parade was an unusually long time in forming, and the citizen soldiery, unaccustomed to the hot uniforms in which they were incased, fell on all sides, prostrated from the heat.

There were military units in the parade representing the States of New York, Massachusetts, Georgia, North Carolina and South Carolina, many of them dating back to Revolutionary days. Each of these units was arrayed in its distinctive uniform, and each of them proudly waved aloft an individual banner inscribed with its name. As the Charleston companies passed the writer, who witnessed the brilliant spectacle, the names on these banners—such as, the German Artillery, the German Fusiliers, the Irish Volunteers, the Lafayette Artillery, historic military units now reorganized as clubs—impressed him with the fact that old Charleston had once been a "melting-pot of nations."

It is a coincidence worthy of note that June 28, 1876, as an important date in the history of South Carolina, possesses a twofold significance. Not only was it the centennial of the victory at Fort Moultrie, but it was also the day on which the first steps were taken in the political revolution of 1876—a most momentous event in the history of the State—a great struggle where the white people, rising in their might, threw off the yoke of carpetbag government and negro domination, which, at the close of the War of Secession, the Republican party of the North had fastened upon them with the aid of Federal bayonets.

(1)

The late R. Means Davis, who was afterwards professor of
history and political economy at the University of South Carolina, was on the staff of the Charleston *News and Courier* in
June, 1876, and later in the year he became assistant secretary
of the State Democratic Executive Committee. He says in
an unpublished manuscript: "June 28 was the Centennial of
Fort Moultrie, and it was determined to celebrate it with great
splendor in a military and civic procession. It was determined
also to inject some politics generally into it by using the memories of the Confederacy, and bringing Hampton . . . to
command. Governor Chamberlain was also honored with a
prominent place in line. . . . The June celebration gave the
ball a great impetus."

General C. Irvine Walker, of Charleston, also notes the political significance of the centennial celebration in Charleston in
1876: "The Palmetto Guard Rifle Club had determined on a
grand parade on the 28th June, 1876, celebrating the centennial
of the Battle of Fort Moultrie. It was always supposed that,
joined with a pariotic intention of celebrating that great historical event, there was an equally patriotic effort, aimed to
secure an equally important and decisive battle for the White
Man's right; . . . it was of vast importance to make a very
powerful demonstration of the white civilization of our State.
When the enthusiastic thousands, in military array, headed by
the immortal Hampton, leading the old war horses of the Confederacy, were seen again, all solidly tramping. . . . It was
the first grand demonstration of that magnificent campaign
which terminated in the redemption of South Carolina."[1]

At that time the Democratic party in South Carolina was
about equally divided in opinion as to whether a "straightout"
ticket, so-called, should be nominated for the approaching election, or whether a coalition should be formed with D. H.
Chamberlain, the Republican Governor, who was a candidate
for re-election, and who had made a more satisfactory Governor than his Republican predecessors. The question was
merely one of expediency, since the party was thoroughly
united on all other issues.

In the light of subsequent events, it is exceedingly difficult
to realize, in this day and time, that, at the beginning of the
year 1876, a majority of the Democratic party in the State

[1]The Carolina Rifle Club (pamphlet), p. 43.

favored a coalition with Chamberlain. The explanation is found in the conditions existing at that time. The Republicans in the State outnumbered the Democrats so greatly that many of the very best men thought that a straightout Democratic candidate for Governor would stand no chance of election and that it would be better that the fight be made to win the Legislature because there the chance of success was better and because only with a decent Legislature could a Governor remedy many of the evils. To show how the most patriotic men differed on the question, suffice it to say that the leaders of the coalition movement, which waned as the year advanced, were such men as J. B. Kershaw, James Conner, Johnson Hagood, John Bratton, and J. D. Kennedy, all recently generals of the Confederate Army—men whose Democracy was unquestioned, and whose character was above reproach. The opposition, that is, those who advocated the straightout movement, which soon began to gain strength in the State, was led by such men as Generals M. C. Butler, M. W. Gary, and W. H. Wallace, and Colonels A. C. Haskell and J. N. Lipscomb—also lately of the Confederate army and whose character and Democracy were equally above reproach.

Governor Chamberlain was a native of Massachusetts, and had been a lieutenant of a negro regiment in the Federal army during the war. As he expressed it "he carried his sword to the South, and when the war was over, remained there." Chamberlain will go down in the history of the State as the human paradox of the Reconstruction era, the enigma which has never been explained. His career was one of such strange contradictions, and the elements were so mixed in him, that he affords rich material for character study and the analysis of motive. An honor graduate of Yale, and an able lawyer, Chamberlain was a gentleman and a scholar in the common acceptation of that term. He was a handsome man, and possessed a strong personality. As a terse and forceful writer of English, he had few equals in his day, while his oratorical powers were of the highest order. Having taken an active part in the venal carpetbagger-negro government, he acknowledged, in after years, that his hope of elevating the recently freed negro by giving him the ballot had proved a delusion. Professor Davis says that Chamberlain "was a brilliant man, cold and impassive, with chiselled features and a smile which always seemed to me of special sweetness."[2]

The evident purpose in inviting Hampton and Chamberlain to Charleston was to give them a tryout. General Hampton was mounted upon a beautiful charger. As chief of cavalry in Lee's army, there was no finer horseman in the South, and, with his commanding figure, he presented a striking appearance as he rode in line, applause greeting him on every hand. Chamberlain, riding in a carriage with distinguished citizens in a prominent place in the parade, was also cordially received.

The public exercises of the day other than the parade were held on Sullivan's Island, amid patriotic surroundings rendered famous in song and story, and well calculated to stir the audience with their mute but eloquent reminders of the past. It is there that "Moultrie holds in leash her dogs of war." In the foreground,

> "Dark Sumter, like a battlemented cloud,
>   Looms o'er the solemn deep";

while on the far edge of the horizon,

> "Old Charleston looks from roof and spire and dome
>   Across her tranquil bay."

Governor Chamberlain who had been invited to deliver the opening address at the formal ceremonies, spoke with his accustomed grace.

General (afterwards Judge) J. B. Kershaw, who was the orator of the day, closed his eloquent address in these stirring words: "Citizens of South Carolina: In this day of bitter humiliation and dire distress, let not these sanguine dreams of the future seem to you but a bitter mockery of your woe—your unutterable wrongs. Truth and justice are eternal, and always bring compensations for transitory interruptions of their free course. The day of wrong and misrule, I fully believe, is passing away—the day of deliverance is at hand. Let the scions of that old Revolutionary stock of the South still display that godlike fortitude that endures unmerited and irremediable wrong as true manhood always endures unavoidable and insuperable calamity, with faith, courage and patience!"

---

[2]Davis' manuscript.

The speaker, with his becoming gray hair and his fine aquiline profile, and with his blue eyes flashing as he pronounced his eloquent peroration, looked every inch a soldier; and the writer, who had the good fortune to be present, was, like everyone else in the vast audience, thrilled with the spirit of the occasion. General Kershaw's brilliant oration met with rounds of applause throughout its delivery. When the applause at its conclusion had subsided, the speaker came again to the front, and said: "Since concluding my remarks to you gentlemen, it has struck me that a certain portion of them, in which I alluded to the sad political conditions of our State, might have been misunderstood and accepted as a reflection upon my honored friend who sits here today (pointing to Governor Chamberlain). Let me assure him and you that my language is carefully worded, and, if it is closely examined, it will be seen that my remarks refer to the condition of the State prior to the time that Governor Chamberlain assumed charge of its interests." (Great applause.) Governor Chamberlain then came to the front of the platform, and said, with inimitable grace: "Gentlemen, it is needless for me to say that I have detected nothing in the words of General Kershaw that I do not recognize as the sincere utterance of a true heart. I could not expect—indeed, it is impossible, that General Kershaw, so brave upon the battlefield of war, could be unjust upon the peaceful field of this day." (Immense cheering.)

This interchange of amenities between the two former soldiers, representatives, the one of South Carolina, and the other of Massachusetts, descendants, respectively, of the Cavalier and the Puritan and each seeming to vie with the other in courtesy and consideration, left an indelible impression upon the minds of all who heard them.

In Charleston that night at a banquet in Hibernian Hall, Major G. Lamb Buist, commanding officer of the Palmetto Guard Rifle Club, of Charleston, who were the hosts of the occasion, presided with General Hampton on his right and Governor Chamberlain on his left. Chamberlain responded to the toast, "The State of South Carolina," while Hampton responded, in person, to that of "Wade Hampton." Both speakers were particularly eloquent in their remarks, and they were both greeted with enthusiasm.

The coalition idea, however, did not wax stronger after the celebration at Fort Moultrie. On the contrary, the straight-out movement gained such impetus throughout the State that it eventually prevailed, with the result that the Democratic Convention which met in Columbia on August 15–16, 1876, nominated a full State ticket with Hampton at its head. The solitary difference which had existed in the Democratic ranks was, from that time forth, completely forgotten, and the party presented a solid front against the enemy. The campaign which ensued was bitter beyond description. Both parties claimed the victory, and both Hampton and Chamberlain were inaugurated as Governor, each by his own adherents. The story of the final victory of the Democrats, when the Federal troops were withdrawn from the State House in Columbia on Tuesday, April 10, 1877, at 12 o'clock, noon, is one of the most thrilling in history.

After the lapse of half a century nearly every one of the leading actors in the stirring drama of 1876 has passed away. Indeed, there are few persons left who were old enough then to recall now many of its chief incidents, while the younger generation are in ignorance of the story, and only know of the general results which are to be gathered from encyclopedias and histories. On the eve, therefore, of the celebration of the semicentennial of this outstanding event in the annals of South Carolina, it seems timely to review the story in that dispassionate manner which the lapse of time renders possible, and without the desire or the intention of reviving any of the unfortunate bitterness which once divided our great country, now happily reunited.

CHAPTER II

IN THE WAKE OF WAR

In order to appreciate to the fullest extent the importance of the political revolution of 1876 in South Carolina, reference should be had to the period of Reconstruction which immediately followed the close of the War of Secession. The depths of suffering and despair to which the people of the State were reduced by that war and its aftermath cannot be expressed in mere words. In proportion to her means, South Carolina contributed more in blood and treasure to the war than any of the Southern States. With a voting population of about 75,000 the State furnished about 85,000 soldiers, 40,000 of whom were killed or injured—the flower of her young manhood.

Early in the war (November, 1861), the Union forces captured the district of Beaufort and the sea-islands off the southern coast of the State, and they controlled that territory unmolested until the close of the war. In many respects that section suffered more from the war than any other part of the State. The white people retreated to the interior, where many of them remained refugees for the greater part of the war. Their abandoned plantations were confiscated by the United States government during their absence, and turned over to the negroes. The entire region was devastated by the enemy, and their homes and outbuildings were burned to the ground.[3]

The capture of the Beaufort section and the siege and bombardment of Charleston were the only military operations of consequence in the State until early in 1865. After the capture of Fort Sumter by the Confederates at the outbreak of the war (April, 1861), Charleston harbor was blockaded until the close of hostilities in 1865; so that the city began to experience the deadening effects of the war from its beginning. The blockade became later a regular siege with the city shelled continuously. All the churches and many of the houses in the lower part of the city were demolished.[4] The correspondent of the *New York Times* reported in the spring of 1864 that fourteen parallel streets in the lower part of the city were deserted,

---

[3]John Porter Hollis, *Early Period of Reconstruction in South Carolina*, p. 12.
[4]*Ibid.*, p. 11.

and that as many as five hundred homes had been struck by shells. "But though the Federals gained one fortification after another until only Fort Sumter remained in the hands of the Confederates, the city stood out heroically against the siege for 576 days, or until February 20, 1865."[5] Then, Sherman having advanced in the rear of Charleston and entered Columbia, the Confederate forces in Charleston, to prevent their capture, retired from the city, which had been reduced to its last extremity by blockade, bombardment and devouring flames.

William Gilmore Simms, the well-known South Carolina author, thus writes of the situation in Charleston immediately following the war: "But no language can describe the suffering which prevails, especially among the class entitled to better days, when pride compels them to *starve in silence.*[6] There are some hundreds in this city who are daily making a sale of such remnants of plate, crockery, furniture, etc., as has been left there to provide daily bread, and there are few of us who do not require the exertion of every hour, far into the night, to keep our heads above water."[7]

South Carolina had been stigmatized by her enemies as "the nest wherein was hatched the snake of Secession," and now these enemies seemed determined that special retribution should be meted out to her unfortunate people. "As a memorable event in South Carolina the Sherman raid is perhaps without a parallel."[8] When everything else in regard to him has been lost in oblivion, Sherman's name will be remembered for the thorough manner in which he exemplified in South Carolina the truth of his epigram, "War is Hell!"

Sherman says in his Memoirs[9]: "Somehow our men have got the idea that South Carolina was the cause of all our troubles; her people were the first to fire on Fort Sumter, had been in a great hurry to precipitate the country into civil war, and therefore on them should fall the scourge of war in all its worst form." The *New York Times* said editorially on December 22, 1864: "Sherman's soldiers are intensely anxious to be led into South Carolina. They are eager beyond measure to take a promenade through the 'Rattle-Snake State.' . . .

[5]*Charleston Courier,* April 18, 1865; Hollis, p. 11.
[6]Italics in original.
[7]W. P. Trent's Life of William Gilmore Simms, p. 296.
[8]Hollis, p. 19.
[9]Vol. II, p. 222.

We do not wonder at it. . . . South Carolina is the guiltiest of all the rebel States. . . . It was South Carolina that incited and forced the other States to disunion; it was South Carolina that passed the first Ordinance of Secession; it was South Carolina that began the war."

With an army of 60,000 men Sherman crossed the Savannah River and entered South Carolina on February 1, 1865. His route was in the direction of Columbia, after he had overrun Beaufort and that part of the State which is included in its southern angle.[10]

The resources of the State, already depleted to the utmost by the ravages of war, were now called upon to subsist this vast horde of marauders, together with some 40,000 horses and mules which were used in the army.[11] Ruthlessly laying waste on every hand with fire and sword, and looting thoroughly the territory through which they passed, the avengers destroyed everything of value that they could not take away with them.

The special correspondent of the *New York Times* writes[12]: "South Carolina has indeed felt the oppressor's heel. Sherman passed through the State, and made a track forty miles wide, as plain as fire, plunder and other devastation could make it. In many places the only marks of former life are the chimneys left standing to tell where once gathered happy families."

General O. O. Howard, U. S. A., who was afterwards Commissioner of the Freedman's Bureau, testifies: "I went over the country afterwards, and it was pretty completely cleaned out. I saw the chimneys, and [there was] scarcely anything left in the country through there."[13]

Simms writes: "The people, both black and white, were left to starve. The only means of subsistence to thousands but lately in affluence was the garbage left by the abandoned camps of the Federal army, and stray corn scraped up from the spots where army horses and mules had been fed."[14]

When Sherman reached Columbia on February 17, nearly three-fourths of the entire place was committed to the flames. The city contained 120 squares, 84 of which were totally de-

---

[10]*Hollis,* p. 114; Appleton's Annual Cyclopedia, 1865, p. 42.
[11]*New York Times,* April 8, 1865.
[12]September 27, 1865.
[13]James G. Gibbes, Who Burned Columbia? p. 105.
[14]Simms' Sack and Destruction of Columbia, p. 22.

stroyed, with scarcely the exception of a single house. The
burnt district extended from Cotton Town, the northern suburb,
to Pendleton Street on the South, and from Bull to Main
Streets, east and west. With the exception of three small
buildings, Main Street was wiped out for twelve blocks. The
burned buildings numbered 1386, and included the old capitol,
four churches, and the Roman Catholic convent, where crowds
of women and children had sought sanctuary with the nuns.[15]
Under date of March 18, the *New York Herald* correspondent
compares the depredations of Sherman's army with those of
the famous barbarian who in the middle ages ravaged southern
Europe. "I will simply observe that the night of Friday,
February 17, would have cracked Alaric's brain if he had witnessed it."[16]

No French or Belgian city presented at the hands of the
Germans during the World War a more perfect protrayal of
"the abomination of desolation" than did the devoted capital
of the State which had been singled out by the conquerors for
their special vengeance.

The loss incurred in the sack and burning of Columbia was
greatly increased by the fact that it was the general impression
that Sherman's march would be through Charleston, and, hence,
Columbia was filled with refugees from the low-country, and
with valuable personal property sent there for safe-keeping—
bank assets and other articles of value, such as silver plate,
jewels, bonds and works of art.[17]

"Having utterly ruined Columbia"[18] the victorious army,
which had met with little or no resistance from the time that it
had crossed the Savannah, moved northward to Winnsboro, and
from there, notheastward. Still spreading desolation in its
track, the invading host crossed the State line, near Cheraw,
and entered North Carolina on March 8. The country which
it left in its wake was scarcely recognizable.

As an evidence of the thoroughness with which the army
performed its work, it may be stated that when destroying

[15]Simms' Sack and Destruction of Columbia, p. 57; *New York Herald,* June 28,
1865.
[16]Singularly enough, Sherman, in writing to an ante-bellum friend in Charleston
in the latter part of 1864, had already compared himself to Alaric. Little did
either of them think at the time of their friendship, he remarks in this letter,
that he (Sherman) would some day be at the head of "a vast army, pointing
like the swarms of Alaric, toward the plains of the South."
[17]Simms, p. 57, *et sequa.*
[18]Sherman's Memoirs, Vol. II, p. 288.

railroad tracks, the engineering corps were provided with ap-
pliances for twisting the rails so that they could not be used
again. Sherman says in his Memoirs:[19] "As soon as we
struck the railroad, details of men were set to tear up the rails,
to burn the ties, and twist the bars." The writer recalls seeing
these rails festooned like gigantic corkscrews around trees and
telegraph-poles all along the railroad right of way, producing
a weird and grotesque effect, which heightened materially the
dismal appearance of the landscape.

The poverty in Columbia after Sherman had swept through
it was something unspeakable—not that genteel poverty from
which the people afterwards suffered, but poverty which meant
actual hunger. There was little to eat or wear, there were no
stores, and, had there been, the people had no money with
which to buy things since the Confederate currency, the only
money they had seen for some years, had become worthless.[20]
Little children were limited to the shortest possible rations,
while their elders suffered in silence. The Freedman's Bureau
was issuing government rations to all who would take the oath
of allegiance; but, for the better class of white people that
alternative was literally as if it had not existed, for it meant
disloyalty to their cause, hopeless as that cause seemed to
them.

Men and women alike bent every energy to the production
of enough food to sustain life, and by their industry and
economy they managed, as a rule, to cope with the situation.
Some of the physically weaker, however, perished for lack of
proper food. Among the number was Henry Timrod, the
poet, who died in Columbia in October, 1867.

Some time before his death, Timrod wrote to Paul H. Hayne,
the poet: "You ask me to tell you my story for the last year.
I can embody it all in a few words: *Beggary, starvation,
death, bitter grief, utter want of hope!* [21] Both my sister and
myself are completely impoverished. We have lived for a
long period, and are still living, on the proceeds of the gradual
sale of furniture and plate. We have—let me see—yes, we

---

[19]Vol. II, p. 259.
[20]"Everything to eat and everything to wear was consumed and when the war
suddenly ended there was nothing left but absolute poverty and nakedness.
Famine followed and suffering beyond computation, the story of which has never
been told."—Pike's Prostrate State, p. 117.
[21]Italics are the poet's.

have eaten two silver pitchers, one or two dozen silver forks, several sofas, innumerable chairs, and a huge—bedstead![22]

Soon after Sherman's march through South Carolina the Confederacy collapsed and the war came to an end. The picture of desolation which greeted the broken soldier, who, after months and years of service in the army, returned, hungry, ragged and foot-sore to his ruined home, affords a background for the period of Reconstruction which followed close on the heels of the war. There was no government of any kind except that of martial law. Hon. A. G. Magrath, Governor of the State, had been arrested on a charge of high treason and imprisoned at Fort Pulaski, Savannah. General Q. A. Gillmore, U. S. A., with headquarters at Hilton Head, in Beaufort County, had command in the State. Lawless men of both races threatened a condition of terror, almost of chaos.

---

[22]Paul H. Hayne, Memoir of Henry Timrod, p. 45.

CHAPTER III

The President Attempts Reconstruction

With the termination of hostilities, the acute question for the Federal authorities to determine was the method of reorganizing the civil governments of the several Southern States.

President Lincoln and Andrew Johnson, who succeeded to the Presidency upon the assassination of Lincoln on April 15, 1865, held practically the same views in regard to the reconstruction of the South. First, both believed that the Constitution and the laws of the United States placed upon the President the duty of Reconstruction. Second, they held that the States which attempted to secede had never actually been out of the Union, and that their efforts to leave it had devolved upon these states only two necessary conditions (beyond the renewal of their allegiance), for restoring their relations to the Union, namely their voiding of all legislation incident to secession, and their acceptance of the emancipation of their slaves. Thus it will be seen that neither Lincoln nor Johnson regarded as necessary to Reconstruction the giving of universal suffrage to the recently freed negro. In fact, both publicly declared they did not favor doing so.

Lincoln's hold upon the people of the North was such that had he lived he would probably have been able to carry through his plan of Reconstruction and the South would thus have been spared a period, the horrors of which were even worse than those of the war. "All the misfortunes of the war itself are insignificant when compared with the sufferings of the people during the era of Reconstruction—1865–1877."[23] But Johnson faced a most trying situation. He was a man of high character and signal ability, who, though a Southerner and a life-long Democrat, had refused to follow his section into secession, and had been nominated for Vice-President on a "Union ticket" with Lincoln, for the purpose of uniting the Republican voters and the Democratic voters who favored a vigorous prosecution of the war. Yet, because he was a Southerner and a Democrat, Johnson never had the trust of the Republicans. The radical Republicans who wished to impose upon the South harsh

[23]The Encyclopedia Britannica, Vol. 25, p. 504.

measures after peace, and yet could hardly have successfully challenged Lincoln, were quite willing to try their strength with Johnson.

In accordance with the Presidential plan, Johnson issued, on May 29, 1865, a proclamation of general amnesty pardoning all who had served the Confederacy, either in military or civil capacity, upon their taking an oath of allegiance to the United States, except certain classes, who, on account of their prominent activities, or for other reasons, were, in his judgment, more culpable. From the excepted classes an individual might make application directly to the President for pardon, whereupon each case would be considered on its merits. Soon afterwards Johnson issued several other proclamations, each providing in the same terms for the Reconstruction of a seceding State, except in the cases of Virginia and Tennessee, where conditions were somewhat different. In each of these proclamations a Provisional Governor for the State was named, and one of his first duties was to arrange for calling a convention for the purpose of altering or amending the Constitution of the State to conform to the changed conditions following the war. Qualification for voting for delegates to, or for serving as a delegate in, the convention was confined to those who had been pardoned under the amnesty proclamation and who were qualified to vote under the laws of the State in force when the State seceded.

As the time for making individual application for pardon under the amnesty proclamation had been short, many leading men were as yet disqualified, but the way was still open for them to qualify. The proclamations of the President gave much satisfaction to the South, for they left the governing of the states to the white people.

The proclamation regarding South Carolina, dated June 30, 1865, named as Provisional Governor, Benjamin F. Perry, of Greenville. Governor Perry was a man of unimpeachable character, who had been conspicuous in the public affairs of South Carolina, and whose ability was well recognized. By this appointment and the other acts of the President already described, the people of South Carolina were warranted in the hope for better things.

Governor Perry's administration was greatly hampered by the presence of a Federal garrison which had been quartered in the State to preserve order, for in this way the government partook somewhat of a dual nature, a condition that frequently brought about conflict of jurisdiction. The fact that the garrison was composed largely of negro troops increased the gravity of the situation, as the negro soldiers were so insolent and arrogant, and their presence in uniform so inflamed the minds of the freedmen, that there were frequent breaches of the peace which made riots between the races imminent. After many appeals from Governor Perry, however, the negro troops were finally withdrawn from the interior of the State and sent to the black districts on the coast.

"The Provisional Governorship of South Carolina was remarkable in one respect—Governor Perry's administration neither received nor paid out one dollar! He was authorized to levy a tax and sell public property, but he declined to do either, as the whole state was poverty stricken."[24] It is of interest to compare Perry's administration in this respect with those of the Governors of the State elected later under the Congressional plan of Reconstruction.

Shortly before Congress met in December, General U. S. Grant, at the request of the President (Johnson) made a tour of inspection in the South. He traveled through South Carolina, and spent two days in Charleston. In his report to the President, he said: "The presence of black troops, lately slaves, demoralizes labor. . . . White troops generally excite no opposition, . . . the late slave seems to be imbued with the idea that the property of his late master should belong to him, or at least should have no protection from the colored soldier. . . . There is danger of collision being brought on by such causes . . . I am satisfied that the mass of the thinking men of the South accept the present situation of affairs in good faith. The questions which have heretofore divided the sentiment of the people of the two sections—slavery and States' Rights, . . . they regard as having been settled forever by the highest tribunal—arms—that man can resort to . . . My observation leads me to the conclusion that the citizens of the Southern States are anxious to return to self-government within the Union as soon as possible.

In addition to the civil and the military governments in the distracted State during Governor Perry's administration, there

[24]Biography of Governor Perry in Perry's Reminiscences of Public Men, p. 17.

existed also the Freedmen's Bureau, which was an independent form of government in itself, and was, in some respects, over the heads of both of the others.[25]   The Bureau, which became a prolific source of conflict between the two races, was a division of the War Department organized early in 1865 for the purpose of protecting the freedmen in their relations with the whites.   The headquarters of the Bureau in South Carolina were at Beaufort.

The chief functions of the Freedmen's Bureau were relief work among both white and black, the administration of justice where the interests of the freedman was concerned, the regulation of labor contracts between him and the white man, and the care of his education.[26]   While the work of the Bureau was productive of some good, there can be no question that, in many respects, its activities were positively harmful.   The higher officials of the Bureau were very good men, as a rule, but most of the subordinate officers and agents were of inferior calibre—fanatics from the North and hangers-on of the army, and many of the latter possessed neither character nor a sense of responsibility.   These undesirable outsiders proceeded on the assumption that the newly freed slaves and their former masters were natural enemies, and often stirred up mischief by giving "the wards of the nation" bad advice, preaching an impossible social equality, and arousing generally hatred between the races.[27]

The power exercised by the Freedmen's Bureau discharging the functions of civil government where the negroes were concerned, was almost despotic, and the Bureau aroused the cordial hatered of the whites by its acts of petty tyranny and oppression.[28]   "The Bureau agents had authority to order the arrest and imprisonment of any citizen on the single statement of any vicious negro and if resistance was made to the mandate of the Bureau agent, the post commander, or military governor, was always ready to enforce it with a file of bayonets."[29]

The negroes were encouraged in the belief that all the land belonged to them.   Some of the more unscrupulous of the Bureau agents were responsible for the hoax that every negro

[25]Walter L. Fleming, Documents Relating to Reconstruction, p. 3.
[26]Ibid.
[27]Ibid.
[28]Ibid., p. 5.
[29]Ku Klux Report—Minority—p. 441.

head of a family who went to the polls and voted the Republican ticket would receive "forty acres and a mule." For years after the war, this hoax was generally believed by the negroes throughout the State, and it induced the more shiftless of the race to conclude that it was not necessary for them to work at all, as the government would take care of them. There are a number of well-authenticated incidents where swindlers from the North did a thriving business among the more ignorant negroes by selling them red and blue pegs at a dollar apiece which were to be used in staking off their "forty acres." These enterprising salesmen assured their ignorant dupes that they might stick these pegs wherever they pleased, and that, after the election, they could claim the land thus staked off— that no one would dare interfere with the pegs, as they had been purchased from the government at considerable expense.[30]

The Bureau agents took an active part in politics from the beginning, and built up the Republican party in the South.[31] In fact, that was largely the reason for which they were sent there. The officers and agents of the Bureau constituted the white membership in the South of the Union League, a political organization formed among the Republicans of the North during the war, and claiming for its main purpose the preservation of the Union.[32] They began at an early period after the war to initiate the negroes into that organization, which became popularly known in the South as the Loyal League. The forerunner of all the political secret societies in the South, its chief object in that section was to keep the white man under foot. Practically all the negroes in the South were members of the League, which taught them in its printed literature that their former masters were their worst enemies, and would put them back into slavery if the Democratic party came into power.[33] The negroes were initiated with much form and with rites which appealed to their superstitious fears, and they were bound by the most solemn obligations to go to the polls and vote the Republican ticket, "shunning the Democratic party as they would the overseer's lash and the auction block."[34] A white person who incurred the enmity of the League was apt

---

[30]Davis' manuscript; Fleming, pp. 44–45.
[31]Fleming, p. 5.
[32]Ibid., pp. 3–5.
[33]Ibid.

to have his house or barn burned in the night-time, and he was without any redress, as the ruling powers were all against him.

Members of the League who incurred its displeasure were persecuted, whipped, and in some cases put to death. Meetings were held at night, the members attending with guns and going through drills, to the terror of the more timid, particularly in communities where the whites were few. In fact, in South Carolina, the Loyal League, in course of time, came simply to mean the negro militia.[35]

By these methods the alien white leaders who came into the State were enabled to dominate the ignorant race, and vote them solidly for the Republican ticket for several years.[36] On election day the military of the league would capture and surround the polls and run the election as they pleased, stuffing the ballot boxes freely whenever they deemed it necessary.[37]

In Reconstruction days the Republicans were known in the South as Radicals, the two terms being used interchangeably. In the same way, the Democrats were known as Conservatives. In the catechism of the Loyal League, which the negroes were made to memorize, is found the following dialogue:

Q. What is the difference between Radicals and Republicans?

A. None. The word Radical was applied to the Republican party by its enemies, and has been accepted by it.

With the restoration of South Carolina to the Union in 1868, most of the officers of the Freedman's Bureau became office-holders under the carpetbag government, and their pernicious activities were thus transferred to other fields. The operations of the Bureau practically ceased then, as "there was no reason for continuing an institution for the protection of a people who exercised entire political control in the State."[38] The offspring of the Bureau, the Loyal League, went out of existence about the same time, but it had accomplished the chief purpose for which it had been instituted—the permanent alienation of the two races by its gospel of hate.

Acting under the proclamation of the President, Governor Perry had called a convention for amending the State Constitution, which assembled in the Baptist Church on Plain Street (now Hampton Avenue), in the city of Columbia, on

[34]Fleming, pp. 3–5.
[35]Ibid, p. 4.
[36]Ibid.
[37]Ibid.
[38]Hollis, p. 128.

September 13, 1865. Hon. James L. Orr, who was a delegate from Anderson, in an address made during the progress of the convention, voiced the sentiment of the people of the State when he said that "President Johnson had interposed the shield of the Constitution between the South and the radicals at the North, and they [the people of South Carolina] should do their part to aid him in his efforts to secure civil rights to the State."[39]

The amendments to the State Constitution which were adopted met with the approval of the President and of the people of the State. Slavery in the State was abolished, the courts were reopened, provision was made for an election for State officers and members of the Legislature. This election, under the same qualification as governed the election for the Constitutional, was held on October 18. "Wade Hampton had long been a leading citizen of South Carolina. At the close of the war, he was regarded as the first man in the State. A general call came for him to accept the office of Governor, but he declined to run, expressing the belief that someone not so closely connected with the armed clash would be more useful than he in restoring the State."[40] Hampton, notwithstanding this position, was voted for so generally, however, that James L. Orr, who was the only candidate for the office, was elected over him by a very small majority.

The newly elected General Assembly met in Columbia on October 25, the Senate holding its sessions in the library of the South Carolina College and the house in the college chapel. The Thirteenth Amendment for the abolition of slavery was ratified, and on December 21 the President relieved Governor Perry of his duties, and directed him to turn his office over to Governor Orr. Reconstruction on the Presidential plan then seemed to be complete.

---

[39]*Charleston Courier*, September 22, 1865.
[40]Davis' manuscript.

CHAPTER IV

CONGRESS UNDERTAKES RECONSTRUCTION

When Congress met in December, 1865, a bitter quarrel in regard to Reconstruction arose between the President and Congress, that body being led by such radicals as Thaddeus Stevens, of Pennsylvania, in the house and Oliver P. Morton, of Indiana, in the Senate. The argument generally advanced by the radical Republicans was that the "rebellion" had destroyed the political status of each of the seceding States— that it was the duty of Congress, and not of the President, to restore the status, and that for this purpose, Congress could impose upon the States whatever conditions it pleased. As the best means for restoring the body politic, it was urged that Congress should reconstruct it largely from the loyal population of each State, which meant the negro.

Congress proceeded with the evident intention of overriding the President's plan, and of placing the South completely under negro domination. Stevens voiced the sentiment of the majority in Congress when, referring to the State governments set up in the South by the President, he said that they "should take no account of the aggregation of white-wash rebels, who, without any legal authority, have assembled in the capitals of the late rebel States and simulated legislative bodies."

South Carolina, in common with other Southern States, was confronted with a tremendous problem in "the sudden catastrophic liberation of this mass of negroes from slaves to freedmen." The States had, therefore, adopted in November, 1865, certain laws for the regulation of labor, and for the government and protection of the 4,000,000 negroes in the South, "lately slaves, now free, ignorant, helpless, brutal, demoralized and dangerous."[41] The United States Census taken a few years later showed that there were only 289,667 white people in the State as against 415,814 negroes.[42] There were twice as many

---

[41]Fleming, p. 3.
[42]This numerical supremacy of the negro, which had existed for 115 years, gradually grew less after the War of Secession until 1926, when it passed away altogether. In that year the whites outnumbered the negroes by some 26,000. This was due, partly to the northward movement of the negroes, and partly to the higher mortality among negro children, in comparison with the whites.

negroes as whites in Charleston County, while in Beaufort and Georgetown Counties the ratio of negroes to whites was ten to one. This ratio gradually decreased away from the coast, so that there were nine counties in the upper part of the State with white majorities: Anderson, Chesterfield, Greenville, Lancaster, Lexington, Marion, Oconee, Pickens and Spartanburg.

The laws in regard to the negro, especially the ones relating to vagrancy, while they followed closely statutes already existing in some of the New England States, gave great offense at the North, where the radical Republican leaders denominated them "Black Codes," and professed to see in them an effort on the part of the South to reduce the negroes to another form of servitude. The radicals in Congress seized upon the laws as affording an opportunity for asserting their constitutional view of Reconstruction by overthrowing the Reconstruction which the President had completed, and, at the same time, they used them as a pretext for punishing the South for what they regarded as its contumacy.

The radical Republicans did not immediately abolish the State governments set up by President Johnson, but they refused to recognize their legality and denied seats in Congress to the Senators and Representatives elected by these governments. Then, alleging as their belief that the negro in the South could be protected against the whites only by giving him political rights, they passed through Congress and submitted to all the States for ratification (1866), the Fourteenth Amendment, conferring full citizenship upon the negro, and making it possible for him to vote and serve on juries.

All the Southern States lately in the Confederacy, except Tennessee, refused to ratify this amendment, whereupon Congress, professing great indignation at what it claimed was further evidence of contumacy on the part of the South, took quick steps to bring to full fruition its idea of Reconstruction. In March, 1867, Congress passed over President Johnson's vetoes, and amidst derisive jeers and uproarious shouts of laughter on the part of the Republicans, what were known as the Reconstruction Acts.[43]

Under the Reconstruction Acts the ten Southern States that

---

[43]D. H. Chamberlain, in the *Atlantic Monthly* for April, 1901, wrote that the debates on these measures were "amazing for their confident levity of tone."

had rejected the Fourteenth Amendment were placed under military rule. They were divided into five military districts, with a general of the United States Army in command of each district. It was the duty of the commander to supervise the organization in each State under his jurisdiction of a civil government to take the place of the Johnson government. The Acts disqualified many of the whites from taking part in organizing the new government, and anticipated the Fourteenth Amendment by allowing all negroes to do so.

Despite their claims of constitutional methods and humanitarian motives, the real purpose of the radical Republicans was to break the backbone of the Democratic party by destroying it in the South, and thus to perpetuate the Republican party in the United States.

Senator Henry Wilson, of Massachusetts, who afterwards (1873) became Vice President of the United States, frankly avowed this intention when he said on the floor of the Senate, in reference to one of the Reconstruction measures before Congress: "Pass this bill, and you make the South Republican for all time."

D. H. Chamberlain wrote in the *Atlantic Monthly* for April, 1901: "But it may now be clear to all, as it was then clear to some, that underneath all the avowed motives and all the open arguments [of the radical Republicans] lay a deeper cause than all others—the will and determination to secure party ascendency and control at the South and in the nation through the negro vote. . . . Sentiment carried the day, sentiment of the lower kind—hate, revenge, greed, lust of power; . . . minds never were more ruthlessly set upon a policy than were Stevens and Morton in putting the white South under the heel of the black South."

North and South Carolina constituted the Second Military District, with General Daniel E. Sickles, U. S. A., in command. As the Johnson governments were allowed to continue until the new civil governments were organized, the States presented the singular spectacle of having for a time. dual governments—civil and military. Thus, in South Carolina there were the civil government under Governor Orr, in accordance with the President's plan of Reconstruction, and the military government under General Sickles, in accordance with the Congressional plan. By his strict construction and enforcement of the Reconstruction Acts, General Sickles soon won the name of a military dictator.[44]

Governor Orr was an able executive, but his task was a most difficult one, as he was seriously handicapped by the conflict of the two jurisdictions, to which, of course, was added that of the Freedmen's Bureau.[45]

General Sickles ordered, in October, 1867, a general registration, which recorded 78,982 negroes as qualified voters and only 46,346 whites. So many whites were disfranchised in Beaufort District that only 65 were registered as against 2,506 negroes.

Numerous stories are told showing how utterly incapable the negroes were of understanding the civic duties suddenly thrust upon them. The special correspondent of the *New York Herald* wrote on September 24, 1867: "Many of our new found brethren, in fact nearly all of them, had no idea what registering meant, and as a natural consequence, the most ludicrous scenes transpired. Quite a number brought along bags and baskets 'to put it in,' and in nearly every instance there was a great rush for fear we would not have registration 'enough to go round.' Some thought it was something to eat; others thought it was something to wear; and quite a few thought it was the distribution of confiscated lands under a new name. All were sworn, and several on being asked what was done when they were registered said that 'De gemblin wid de big whisker make me swar to deport de laws of United Souf Calina.' "

Thus, at the point of the bayonet, was evolved a condition which is without parallel in all history—some of the very best and noblest citizens of the State put in a position of political inferiority to the lowest negroes—their recent slaves. Democrats endeavored to have the Supreme Court of the United States pass upon the constitutionality of the Reconstruction Acts, but the radical Congress prevented. By their unwillingness to test the legality of the Acts the Radicals showed that they felt that they had nothing upon which to base their plan of Reconstruction except the law of force—the same law which

[44]Hollis, p. 69.
[45]Governor Orr later united with the Republicans and was, in 1868, elected by them Judge of the Eighth Circuit. He died in 1873, in Russia, where he was serving as American Minister by appointment of President Grant.

had previously settled, adversely to the South, the question of States' Rights.

The power of prescribing the qualifications for voters was one that the several States had reserved to themselves upon the adoption of the Constitution of the United States; and nowhere in that instrument was it provided that the Federal government should exercise that power. The right to vote not having been conferred upon the negro up to this time, he was now permitted to do so solely by the arbitrary mandate of Congress promulgated through General Sickles, who had the whole force of the United States Army at his back.

It will be noted too, that in accepting the State's ratification of the Thirteenth Amendment, and in endeavoring to have it ratify the Fourteenth Amendment, Congress, by implication, admitted that the State had been regularly reconstructed under the Presidential plan, and was a part of the Union; in other words, Congress would have it that the State was in the Union for some purpose, but out of it for others.[46] The position seemed to be that South Carolina and the other Southern States "were competent to vote on the Amendment, but competent to vote only one way."[47]

Immediately following the passage of the Reconstruction Acts the Republican party in South Carolina was formally organized (1867). At the beginning of the control of affairs in the State by the army and the Freedmen's Bureau (1865), a horde of adventurers from the North, white and colored, had swarmed like locusts into South Carolina and the other Southern States. Men utterly without character as a rule, they were contemptuously termed "carpetbaggers," implying that what each owned when he entered the State could have been contained in a carpetbag, or portable travelling bag. Many of them were "hold-overs" from the worst elements of Sherman's army. "As a class they were not nearly the equals of the negroes of the South."[48] These strangers were joined by a few native white renegades, who became known as "scalawags"; and this combination furnished the leaders for the Republican party in South Carolina. While a few native negroes rose to office, the mass of them constituted the rank and file of the Republican party in

[46]Hollis, p. 61.
[47]Ibid., p. 66.
[48]Chamberlain in *Atlantic Monthly* for April, 1901, p. 477.

the State. Naturally the Republicans in South Carolina supported enthusiastically the Reconstruction measures of Congress.

The Democrats, in State and nation, condemned the Reconstruction Acts. Prominent South Carolina Democrats, headed by Wade Hampton, issued (1867) an address in which it was alleged that the Reconstruction Acts placed "the South, politically and socially, under the heel of the negro; and that what was sought by this was not negro equality merely, but negro supremacy."[49]

Later, at the National Democratic Convention in 1868, Wade Hampton denounced the Reconstruction Acts as unconstitutional. The National Democratic platform declared them to be unconstitutional, revolutionary and void, and upon this platform stood the Democratic candidates for President and Vice President, Horatio Seymour, Governor of New York and Frank P. Blair, who had been a distinguished general in the Federal army. Many of the most eminent lawyers of the country, irrespective of their political affiliations, agreed with the Democratic position that the Reconstruction Acts were unconstitutional.

---

[49]Hollis, p. 81; *Charleston Courier*, November 9, 1867.

CHAPTER V

Establishing the Carpetbag-Negro Government

Meanwhile, the time approached for an election in South
Carolina on the question of holding a convention for the purpose of adopting a State Constitution under which a new civil
government should be organized. The registration of voters
had been preparatory to this election. Wade Hampton, in an
open letter, advised everyone to register who was qualified, but
to vote against holding the Convention, maintaining that it
would be better for the State to continue under military rule
than to sanction measures "which we believe to be illegal, unconstitutional and ruinous." Hampton counselled friendliness
and fair-dealing toward the negro, for the negro was in no way
responsible for the condition which existed in the State. If
amicable relations were sustained, he said, the negro would
soon learn to trust his white friends. He further declared
himself as in favor of impartial suffrage, and advocated a Constitution which would give the negro the same right in voting
as the white man. "Alone of all the prominent men in the
State," wrote Chamberlain in 1901,[50] "Hampton, in 1868, publicly advised cooperation with the negro in elections, but his
advice passed unheeded." In addressing some of his old soldiers in Pickens District, in the fall of 1866, General Hampton
said in regard to the negro: "As a slave, he was faithful to
us; as a freedman, let us treat him as a friend."

Until the coming of the carpetbaggers, there had been no
particular animosity between the races, and, generally speaking,
they were on friendly terms. On the part of their former
masters, "for the great mass of the negroes, there was no feeling but kindness, mixed with regret that they should have been
made the instruments of wrongs against which the white people
rebelled."[51]

The two races in the South understood each other, and it is
safe to say that, if they had been left alone to work out their
own salvation under the Congressional plan of Reconstruction,

---

[50]*Atlantic Monthly* for April.
[51]James S. Reynolds, Reconstruction in South Carolina, p. 99.

with such leaders as Wade Hampton to guide them, and without any interference from wicked and designing men from abroad, the outcome would have been vastly different. As has been seen, however, such a result would not have suited the radical Republican leaders of the North, who had other plans for the negro vote.

Waddy Thompson, in A History of the People of the United States,[52] says: "With the Southern soldiers at the front, the slave worked the crop by day, and guarded the women and children by night; or he followed his master into the army, where he cared for the soldier's wants, rejoiced in his victories, and with sorrowing heart brought back to the old homestead the warrior's lifeless body. The slave's faithfulness to his master and to his master's family causes still the admiration of the world."

A handsome monument on the public square at Fort Mill, South Carolina, which was erected with the approval of the Jefferson Davis Memorial Association, bears the inscription:

1860

Dedicated to the faithful slaves, who, loyal to a sacred trust, toiled for the support of the army with matchless devotion, and with sterling fidelity guarded our defenseless homes, women, and children during the struggle for the principles of our Confederate States of America.

1865

But Hampton's advice in regard to voting on the question of the Constitutional Convention also went unheeded. While, as a rule the whites, who were qualified, registered, they adopted generally the policy of refraining from voting—some because they realized that they were in a hopeless minority, and were reduced to despair—others because they considered that the State had already been rehabilitated by the President, and was under the protection of the Constitution of the United States.

There were yet others who regarded the whole proceeding as unconstitutional, and believed that the Supreme Court would so declare it. There were not wanting, too, those who refrained from voting because they hoped that, in this way, the result would show that less than half of those registered had voted, and that thereby the call for the convention would be

[52]P. 369.

defeated; for the law required that for the convention to be held the total vote cast must be a majority of the total registered vote. Those who held this view, however, were doomed to disappointment, for when the election was held (November, 1867) the Constitutional Convention was decided upon affirmatively by the votes of the negroes, *whose right to vote at all, upon any subject whatsoever, was the very question to be settled by the proposed Convention which was to be assembled by their votes!*[53]

By order of General E. R. S. Canby, U. S. A., who had succeeded General Sickles, the Constitutional Convention assembled in Charleston, January 14, 1868, for the purpose of framing a Constitution and civil government. The convention was "dominated by the native negroes and Northerners of both races, who had come into the State as Federal agents and adventurers."[54]

From the varied complexion and nationalities of those who composed its membership, it was known as the "Ring-streaked and Striped Convention." It was composed of 73 negroes and 51 white men, 57 of the negroes having been slaves three years before. Quite a variety of States and nationalities were represented in the body—South Carolina, North Carolina, Georgia, Virginia, Tennessee, Massachusetts, Connecticut, Rhode Island New York, Pennsylvania, Michigan, Ohio, England, Ireland, Denmark, Prussia and Dutch Guiana. The total taxes paid by the 120 Republican members was $359.70, less than $3 apiece; 59 of the negroes and 23 of the whites paid no taxes at all.[55]

"The personnel of the Convention . . . was an index to that of every similar body assembled in the State during the period of negro rule . . . the Constitutional Convention, the General Assembly and every convention of the party. . . . The pervading characteristic of the negro government and its agents was irresponsibility . . . [since they were amenable] neither to the laws, to public opinion, to official obligation, nor to an overlooking constituency."[56]

[53]John J. Hemphill, The Solid South, p. 85.
[54]A. A. Taylor—Negro Republican—The Negro in South Carolina During the Reconstruction.
[55]Reynolds, p. 79.
[56]*Ibid.*, pp. 504-5.

When invited to address it, Governor Orr did not hesitate to say that the Convention was representative only of the colored people of South Carolina; that the intelligence, wealth and refinement of the State had no voice in its deliberations.

D. H. Chamberlain's first appearance in public life in South Carolina was as a member of this Convention. He afterwards wrote of it in the *Atlantic Monthly* for April, 1901: "The property, the education and intelligence, the experience in self-government and public affairs, were, of course, wholly with the white population. Numbers alone were with the rest. . . . It [the Convention] did not contain one Democrat, or one white man who had had high standing in the State previously."[57]

The Constitutional Convention was in session for two months and the Constitution which was adopted remained in force until 1895.[58] During the last week of its session the Constitutional Convention resolved itself into a State Republican Convention, nominating Robert K. Scott, of Ohio, for Governor, and Lemuel Boozer,[59] of Lexington, for Lieutenant Governor, together with a full State ticket, including D. H. Chamberlain for Attorney-General.

The State Democratic Convention assembled in Columbia on April 3, 1868, and issued an address to the colored people, in which they said: "Your leaders, both white and black, are using your votes for nothing but their individual gain. . . . Remember that your race has nothing to gain and everything to lose, if you invoke that prejudice of race, which, since the world was made, has ever driven the weaker tribe to the wall. Forsake then the wicked and stupid men who would involve you in this folly, make to yourselves friends and not enemies of the people of South Carolina."

The *Charleston Mercury* protested editorially: "If it is the purpose of the United States government to negroize the Southern States, they may as well know now that *it has to be done with the bayonet, and has to be preserved with the bayonet in all time to come.*"

---

[57]Reynolds, p. 475.
[58]By the Constitution of 1868 the designation of the political subdivision of the State theretofore known as District was changed to County.
[59]Boozer was a native of Lexington County, a good lawyer and a man of high integrity. He was elected Judge of the Fifth Circuit in 1868, and died, while holding that position, in 1870.

Hon. Armistead Burt, Chairman of the State Democratic Executive Committee, indignantly asserted that "The taxable property is held by one race, and the law-making power by the other. . . . Without any qualifications whatsoever, one class is allowed to vote, while the other is disfranchised. Those who do not hold property vote to make laws, while the property owners are not allowed to vote for even a constable."[60]

A protest against the adoption of the Constitution was submitted to Congress by the Central Committee of the Democratic party in the State, represented by Colonel John P. Thomas, of Columbia, who "carefully and earnestly presented to both Houses of Congress the disastrous results of unqualified negro suffrage." The protests asserted that the new constitution "was the work of Northern adventurers, Southern renegades and ignorant negroes ; . . .   that it enfranchised every male negro over the age of twenty-one, and disfranchised many of the purest and best white men of the State. The negroes being in a large numerical majority as compared with the whites, the new Constitution establishes in this State negro supremacy with all its train of countless evils. . . . We do not mean to threaten resistance by arms, but the people of our State will never quietly submit to negro rule ; . . .   by every peaceful means left to us, we will keep up this contest until we have regained the political control handed down to us by an honored ancestry."[61] This remonstrance was without avail, however, and the Constitution was duly approved by Congress.

At a general election which was held under the new Constitution in April, 1868, the full Republican State ticket was elected. The Democrats had no State ticket in the field, but they made a strong fight for Presidential electors, congressmen and solicitors, with the result that they elected the solicitors in six out of the eight judicial circuits. The vote for Presidential electors stood 62,300 Republican, and 45,137 Democratic.

Democratic Clubs had been organized during the campaign. Efforts to get negroes to join these clubs met with little success. A few negroes did so, but they met with such harsh treatment from members of their own race that others were deterred from following their example. The excited condition of the public

---

[60]*Charleston Mercury*, April 8, 1868; Hollis, p. 102.
[61]Appleton, 1868, p. 697.

mind led to race riots, in which several Republican leaders were killed in different parts of the State.

The Legislature which was elected with Scott ratified the Fourteenth Amendment. As has been seen, however, the majority of that body had itself been elected by the votes of the negroes, *in anticipation of the Amendment's passing and conferring the vote upon the negro!*

Upon approval by Congress of the State's new Constitution and by the ratification by the State of the Fourteenth Amendment, South Carolina was declared by Congress, on June 25, 1868, to be reconstructed and readmitted into the Union—"reconstructed by Federal bayonets and in subordination to the military authority of the United States."[62] In its more generally accepted sense, however, what is known as the Reconstruction period extended to April 10, 1877, the day upon which the Federal troops were removed from the State House in Columbia, and the white people came again into their own.

With the inauguration of Scott, on July 9, 1868, the military rule which had been supreme in South Carolina for more than a year came to an end. Under the military regime the civil authority had been subordinated, the commanding general of the military district having had absolute power. His every mandate was enforced at the point of the bayonet, and his rule, "from first to last, constituted as brutish a tyranny as ever marked a course of any government whose agents and organs claimed to be civilized."[63]

[62]Reynolds, p. 498.
[63]*Ibid.*, p. 98.

CHAPTER VI

THE "BOND RING"

Ill-starred South Carolina passed from bayonet rule to the government of those "who robbed while they pretended to rule; who plundered while they professed to protect." For there now began an orgy of corruption and crime, and the people of the State "entered upon a period of mental anguish and material disaster unequalled in the annals of civilization." South Carolina was one of the last Southern States to throw off the yoke of carpetbag-negro intolerance and its condition during Reconstruction was so much worse than that of the others, that it soon became generally known as "The Prostrate State."

Robert K. Scott, the first Republican Governor of the State, was a practicing physician in Ohio when appointed to the Federal Army, where he rose to the rank of Major General (Brevet) of Volunteers, and served in that capacity in South Carolina with Sherman's army. He became Assistant Commissioner in charge of the Freedmen's Bureau in the State, and resigned from that position and from the army to be inaugurated as Governor.[64]

Scott was the first Governor to reside in the Executive Mansion, and he entertained there negroes and whites, of both sexes, on terms of perfect social equality.[65]

More than half of the legislators elected with Scott were negroes. Most of them had very little education, and some were unable to write their names. The body contained 21 Democrats and 136 Republicans on joint ballot. The total taxes paid by the Republicans in the Legislature was $431.39, or an average of $3.12 apiece; ninety-one of them paid no taxes at all. The succeeding Legislatures during the period of carpet-

[64]Scott was a man of some ability and culture. He had popular manners and considerable shrewdness and common sense. There was an impediment in his speech.

[65]The building now used as the Executive Mansion was remodeled for the purpose. It consisted originally of two apartment houses, for use as officers' quarters of the Arsenal Academy—a preparatory school to the Citadel in Charleston. The Arsenal barracks, situated on the southern portion of the lot occupied by the Executive Mansion, were destroyed by Sherman's army.

The Executive Mansion, for a period of six years succeeding its occupancy by Scott (1872-78) was rented to Mrs. S. L. Wright, of Wright's Hotel fame, who conducted a fashionable boarding house. Simpson was the first Democratic Governor to reside at the Mansion.

TYPICAL SOUTH CAROLINA LEGISLATORS OF 1868

Of the sixty-three members of the Legislature shown in the illustration, fifty were negroes or mulattoes and thirteen were white men. Only twenty-two of the entire number could write their names, the remaining forty-one having to sign with a cross. The total taxes paid by all of them was only $146.10, while forty-four of the number paid no taxes at all. The General Assembly of which these men formed a part levied upon the white people of the State taxes amounting to $4,000,000.

Jillson, the white carpetbagger who was State Superintendent of Education, is the second man in the second row, counting from the left; Beverly Nash, the negro Senator from Richland, is the second man in the fifth row, counting from the left; while Wright, the negro Associate Justice of the Supreme Court, is the first man in the second row counting from the right.

bag and negro domination were of much the same complexion
—political and otherwise—as the first.

A special session of the Legislature assembled on July 6, 1868,
and continued in session for more than two months. Governor
Scott was inaugurated on July 9. F. J. Moses, Jr., a native
South Carolinian who had turned "scalawag," was elected
Speaker of the House. He held at the same time the office of
Adjutant and Inspector General of the State. The Fourteenth
Amendment was promptly ratified by both Houses. The Fif-
teenth Amendment, providing that the right of citizens to vote
should not be denied by any State on account of race, color, or
previous condition of servitude, was ratified at the regular ses-
sion which began in November.[66]

The most interesting chronicle of the carpetbag-negro misrule in the South is found in *The Prostrate State,* written by
James S. Pike, of Maine, who visited South Carolina in the
winter of 1872-73, and thus obtained first-hand impressions of
the conditions existing in the State at the time. Pike was
one of the most distinguished men in the Republican party.
He had been Washington correspondent and associate editor
of the New York Tribune from 1850 to 1860, and had served
as United States Minister to Holland from 1861 to 1866. Extracts from Pike's pungent account of the situation in South
Carolina will show how it impressed this dyed-in-the-wool Republican abolitionist:

"The experience of South Carolina during and since the war
is one of the most tragic episodes in history. When before did
mankind behold the spectacle of a rich, high-spirited, cultivated
self-governed people suddenly cast down, bereft of their pos-
sessions, and put under the feet of the slaves they had held in
bondage for centuries?[67]

"The rule in South Carolina should not be dignified with
the name of government. It is the installation of the highest
system of brigandage. They are men who have studied and
practised the art of legalized theft. They are in no sense
different from, or better than, the men who fill the prisons and
penitentiaries of the world. They are, in fact, officially that
class, only more daring and audacious. They pick your pockets

---

[66]At the special session of the Legislature, in 1868, Thomas J. Robertson, of
Columbia, and Frederick A. Sawyer, of Charleston, were elected United States
Senators.
[67]P. 92.

by law. They rob the poor and the rich alike, by law. They confiscate your estate by law." [68]

"It is the spectacle of a society suddenly turned bottom-side up. . . . In the place of this old aristocratic society stands the rude form of the most ignorant democracy that mankind ever saw invested with the forms of government. . . . It is barbarism overwhelming civilization by physical force. It is the slave rioting in the halls of his master and putting that master under his feet." [69]

"In all modern history there has been no such substitution of ignorance for knowledge, of barbarism for civilization, of stolidity for intelligence, of incapacity for skill, of vice and corruption for probity and virtue." [70]

The corruption which before the end of Reconstruction reached every branch of the State government will never be known in its fullness, but much of it has been set forth in detail in "The Report of the Joint Investigating Committee on Public Frauds," commonly known as the Fraud Report, which was made to the Legislature in 1877-78, after the white people had regained control of the government. This committee, hereafter referred to as the Democratic Legislative Investigating Committee, was composed of members of that party, with the exception of its chairman, Senator John R. Cochran, of Anderson, who was one of the few native Republicans who stood well in the State. The Democratic members of the committee were all men of the highest character and of unblemished reputation. The chief testimony taken by them was that of the Radicals themselves who had participated in the stealing, and most of whom confessed to it without any apparent feeling of shame. In making their investigations the committee had two previous reports to guide them, namely, that of a Joint Select Committee of Congress, dated February 19, 1872, which is hereafter referred to as the Congressional Investigating Committed;[71] and (2) the report of an Investigating Committee (Republican) of the South Carolina General Assembly, hereafter referred to as the Republican Legislative Investigating Committee, which was made at the session of 1871-72.

The wholesale plundering of the State, begun with Scott's

---

[68] Pike, p. 58.
[69] *Ibid*, p. 12.
[70] *Ibid*, p. 82.
[71] A majority of the Congressional Investigating Committee were Republicans.

inauguration and continued uninterruptedly during the entire eight years of carpetbag-negro misrule, was conducted chiefly through regularly constituted rings, which were organized from time to time as the thieving progressed, and were composed of various State officers and members of the Legislature.

The Legislature created in 1868 a Financial Board, consisting of the Governor (Scott), the Attorney General (Chamberlain), and the State Treasurer (Parker).[71a] The Financial Board, together with Comptroller General Neagle and John J. Patterson, later United States Senator, formed the "Bond Ring." This was the first ring to set about the systematic robbery of the State's finances. Its scheme involved the manipulation of the public debt.

The Financial Board employed as its financial agent in New York City Hiram K. Kimpton, of Boston, a former classmate and intimate friend of Chamberlain. Kimpton was probably the most accomplished swindler and the largest beneficiary of Republican stealing in South Carolina, with the possible exception of John J. Patterson.

Kimpton was a past master in the juggling of figures, and would have made a fortune as a latter-day stock salesman. He "affected much style in dress and great elegance of manner— gold-rimmed spectacles being among the accessories used to give him a distinguished appearance; the Charleston *News and Courier* it was that first called him 'cherubic'—so suave and calm and sleek did he always look. He was essentially what would now be known as a 'smooth article.' "[72]

Since Kimpton falsified his accounts with the State as agent for the Financial Board, it is impossible to tell with exactness the extent to which the several members of the "Bond Ring" were involved in the swindle. Kimpton afterwards acknowledged "the incorrectness of his accounts, and admitted that he was directed by the Financial Board not to make real but fictitious entries; so frightfully large were the expenses of the transactions of the agency, in negotiations of loans, etc., the board thought it best to keep the true amounts in disguise." [72a]

[71a]Niles G. Parker, like Chamberlain, was a native of Massachusetts and came to South Carolina in command of a company of negro troops. He had genial manners, but was uncultured, utterly filled with vice, and had neither conscience nor character.

[72]Reynolds, p. 116.

[72a]Kimpton's testimony before the Republican Legislative Investigating Committee in 1871.

But undoubtedly John J. Patterson—"Honest John," as he
was commonly called[73]—was easily the Napoleon of Finance
among the many Captains of Industry who figured prominently
in those dark days for South Carolina. It was Patterson who,
when it was suggested in Moses' administration that the Republican paarty in the State should reform, made answer,
"Why, there are five years more of good stealing in South
Carolina." Patterson, in conspiracy with other members of the
"Bond Ring," manipulated the affairs of the Greenville &
Columbia and the Blue Ridge Railroads so that the State lost
a cool six million dollars, with nothing to show for it. The
details of this deep-laid scheme are too involved and intricate
to be set forth here, but its general plan may be gathered from
the following letter:

"Office of the Attorney-General,
"Columbia, S. C., Jan. 5, 1870.
"My Dear Kimpton—
"Parker arrived last evening and spoke of the G. & C. matter, etc.
I told him that I had just written you fully on that matter, and also
about the old Bk. bills.
"Do you understand fully the plan of the G. & C. enterprise? It is
proposed to buy $350,000. worth of the G. & C. stock. This with the
$433,000. of stock held by the State will give entire control to us. The
Laurens branch will be sold in February by decree of Court, and will
cost not more than $50,000., and probably not more than $40,000. The
Spartanburg and Union can also be got without difficulty.
"We shall then have G. & C. 168 miles, in Laurens 31, and S. & U.
70 miles—in all 269 miles, equipped and running. Put a first mortgage
of $20,000. a mile on this—sell the bonds at 85 or 90, and the balance,
after paying all outlays for cost and repairs, is immense, over $2,000,000
There is a mint of money in this, or I am a fool.
"Then we will soon compel the South Carolina Railroad to fall into
our hands and complete the connection to Asheville, N. C.
"There is an indefinite verge for expansion of power before us.
"Write me fully and tell me of anything you want done. My last
letter was very full.
"Harrison shall be attended to at once. I don't think Neagle will
make any trouble. Parker hates Neagle, and magnifies his intentions.
"Yours truly,
"D. H. CHAMBERLAIN."

The Charleston *News and Courier,* in advocating a coalition
with Chamberlain in 1876, at which time the foregoing letter
was being used against him, suggested that it might have been
a forgery. However, while Chamberlain had every opportunity
in the world of pronouncing it a forgery, he never did so.

[73] "A political associate explained this nickname by saying: 'Patterson will do
what he says. If he promises to pay you, he'll do it; if he promises to vote for
you, he'll do it; if he promises to work for you, he'll do it; and if he promises
to steal for you, he'll do it.' "—Reynolds, p. 229.

In order to procure the legislative enactments necessary to carry through the deal in these railroad bonds, members of the Legislature were freely bribed. Beverly Nash, the negro Senator from Richland, subsequently testified regarding the sale of his vote in the matter: "Afterwards I seen Leslie [white Republican from New York] in one of these rooms, and he handed me a small package, about the size of a brick, which I took and carried home, and on examination found that it contained about $5,000.00 in money."[74]

The taxpayers of the State becoming alarmed on account of the deplorable fiscal condition which existed, held a convention in Columbia in the spring of 1871. Strange to say, Attorney-General Chamberlain attended this convention as a delegate from Richland County, and was elected one of its vice-presidents. The convention adopted a resolution repudiating, as property-holders and taxpayers, the fraudulent issue of State bonds, which they asserted were not binding upon them. Strenuous efforts were made by the convention to bring about some relief from the desperate condition which existed in the State; but these efforts were without avail, and the taxes kept mounting up higher and higher, so that in a single year 243,971 acres of land were forfeited for taxes.

Largely through the manipulations of the Financial Board and its agent, the bonded debt of the State, which was only five million dollars when the Republicans took charge, was increased to over eighteen million in four years. The Governor's message to the Legislature, in the fall of 1871, showed that $3,129,000.00 of the increase of the debt had been saddled on the State within the six months that had ensued since the Taxpayers' Convention, and the State received nothing in return for this gigantic misuse of its credit.

While the "Bond Ring" furnished, in point of time, the first scheme for defrauding the State, soon other methods were evoked, and, as each new method was brought into play, the circle of corruption among the office-holders widened. Naturally, it was not long before some of the money grabbers be-

[74]Testimony before the Democratic Legislative Investigating Committee. 1877-78. Nash, who had been a slave of Colonel William C. Preston, was a strapping black negro, six feet in height. Before going into politics, he had been porter for one of the hotels in Columbia. He was a man of good address, and of considerable native ability, although his education was limited. Nash was quite an orator, and was very violent and incendiary in his harangues. He was the Republican leader in the State Senate, and lorded it over his fellow Republicans in that body, white as well as black. He could tell a good story, and always carried the crowd with him.

came dissatisfied because they believed they were not receiving their full share of the spoils. These disgruntled "statesmen" persuaded the Legislature, in 1871, to appoint a committee, generally known as the Republican Investigating Legislative Committee, to investigate the administration of Governor Scott, although Scott had been elected for another term.

This committee cited many cases of extravagance and fraud and reported, regarding the manipulation of the public debt by the "Bond Ring," that "they do not feel that they can safely say that they have given the full extent of extravagance or criminal indulgence with which the management of the funds and credit of the State has been characterized. * * * The committee, in view of the atrocity of their disclosures—the work of the present administration, or rather a ring composed of leading officers of the State government, unhesitatingly say that the Republican party, which has elected them to power, must * * * bring to justice those who have prostituted the authority with which they have been clothed— * * * must deal with bad men, though they be their acknowledged leaders, as justice demands. * * * We have the indisputable evidence that all the financial officers of the State, as well as the Governor himself, in their State and official papers, have hitherto disguised the true condition of the public debt as well as the issue of bonds."

About this time the joint committee of Congress investigated the condition of affairs in the Southern States. Judge Poland, of Vermont, a member of the committee on the part of the House and a prominent and able Republican, reported to Congress: "The real amount of the debt seems to be an unsettled problem, involving Governor, Treasurer, and State Agent in charges of dishonest and unlawful conduct, and presenting a state of such uncertainty that the existence of the controversy is in itself disgraceful to all these officers, and cannot but be disastrous to the credit and interests of the commonwealth."

The Republican Legislative Investigating Committee having cited in its report a particular case where bonds amounting to more than six million dollars had been fraudulently issued, this case was taken by the legislators who had broken with the administration as the basis for the introduction into the House of resolutions looking to the impeachment of Governor Scott and State Treasurer Parker. Although as much involved as anyone in the machinations of the "Bond Ring," John J. Patterson encouraged the movement for impeachment in order to extort money from Scott.[75] This successful attempt at blackmail would be amusing were it not indicative of the depth to which South Carolina had fallen. Parker told the story in his testimony before the Joint Investigating Committee of the Democratic Legislature (1877-78). He got the facts from Scott and Patterson, both of whom discussed the matter freely with him at the time.

Parker testified that Scott's "fears were greatly aroused, and he became almost frantically excited, and I have every reason in the world to believe that Patterson used every means to alarm him. Patterson told him that unless he paid a large sum of money to the members of the Legislature he would surely be impeached." Patterson finally succeeded in obtaining from Scott his signature to three blank warrants, on what was known as the "Armed Force Fund." They were made out on the Governor's printed forms; the amount in each case was left blank and was to be filled in by Patterson. Scott and Patterson went separately to Parker's office, within half an hour after the agreement had been made, and both informed him of it. Scott said to Parker: "I don't know what amount he [Patterson] will want; I hope not a very large amount, but I suppose the scoundrel will make it as large as he can." Scott then proceeded to denounce Parker roundly, for he said he believed that Parker had done all in his power to put up the impeachment job against him. Parker told Scott that he did not believe that it was necessary to pay a dollar—that the proposed proceedings were simply for the purpose of extorting money from Scott. To this Scott replied: "While I hate to do it, I will not suffer impeachment if it takes every dollar there is in the State Treasury." The blank impeachment warrants were subsequently filled in for an aggregate of $48,645, and were paid by Parker from the State Treasury. Some of the money was used to buy enough votes among the legislators to kill the impeachment resolution; the rest Patterson put in his pocket. Speaker Moses said he received $15,000 for employing a shrewd parliamentary move to block the efforts of the members who had not received any of the money and who started to filibuster against the vote to kill the resolutions.[76]

[75]Fleming, Nos. 4 and 5, p. 35; Reynolds, p. 470.
[76]Moses' testimony before the Democratic Legislative Investigating Committee.

CHAPTER VII

OTHER NOTORIOUS RINGS

The Legislature, at its regular session beginning November 24, 1868, created a land commission, for the purchase of homes for indigent negroes. The advisory board of this commission consisted of Governor Scott, Comptroller General Neagle, State Treasurer Parker, and Secretary of State Cardoza, together with Attorney-General Chamberlain, who was the legal advisor of the board. C. P. Leslie, a carpetbagger from New York, who was State Senator from Barnwell County, was appointed Land Commissioner. Soon this ring was robbing the State. The Republican Legislative Investigating Committee of 1870-71 charged that this commission was "a gigantic folly" whose powers had been used to subserve a certain organized result, viz., the primary benefit of the members of the advisory board and the land commission and their subservient allies.

The State sustained a total loss of about $600,000.00 at the hands of this commission. The fraud here was accomplished by inserting in each deed conveying the property to the State a sum to represent the price paid for the land which was in excess of the price actually paid. One of the deals was the purchase of 17,533 acres in Charleston and Colleton (now Berkeley and Dorchester) counties, known as "Hell Hole Swamp." These lands, which were absolutely worthless for agricultural purposes, cost the State $120,754.00 in Republican times and were finally sold for $7,783.00, or about forty cents an acre.

Another opportunity for filching the people's money was afforded in the furnishing of supplies to members of the Legislature. The flagrancy of this steal may best be gathered from excerpts from testimony of Republicans given to the Democratic Legislative Investigating Committee, and published in the Fraud Reports:

Under the head of supplies was included anything that a legislator chose to order, and these orders increased until they assumed gigantic proportions. The supplies were usually classified as "sundries, stationery, refreshments, carpetings, furniture, jewelry, rents." In this way public officials and members of the Legislature had their private bills paid by the State, and the items included every conceivable article under the sun. Double the amount necessary to pay the bills was usually appropriated, and many of the bills were rendered and paid twice. C. P. Leslie voiced the prevailing sentiment among his colleagues when he said that "South Carolina has no right to be a State unless it can take care of its statesmen." And then he and his brother "statesmen" proceeded to acquire, at the expense of the State, furniture, clothing, groceries, fine horses, mules, carriages, buggies, harness, gold watches and chains, gold breast-pins, diamond pins, pocket-pistols, colognes, French extracts, Florida water, decorated "cuspidores" (sic), wash tubs, ladies' hoods, skirt braid, hooks and eyes, balmoral skirts, bustles, chignons, chemises, extra long stockings, etc., etc., etc. Truly were all the wants of these "statesmen" supplied at the expense of the State "from the cradle to the grave," for, in one instance, a cradle was listed among the articles paid for, while in still another instance a coffin.

By far the largest of the supply bills were for "refreshments," which included the choicest wines, liquors, eatables and cigars furnished to members of the Legislature and their friends in a room which was fitted up luxuriously for that purpose next to the office of the Clerk of the Senate. This room was daily patronized by State officials, judges, lawyers, editors, newspaper reporters and citizens generally. Everything was free of cost to "statesmen" or friends of a legislator or of other office-holders. The room was kept open from eight o'clock in the morning to three or four o'clock on the following morning, and contained the best that money could buy. Some of the "statesmen" would, on leaving, put bottles of champagne and lots of cigars in their pockets as there was nothing to hinder them.

Orders were left there for liquors and cigars to be sent to the hotels, boarding houses, or residences of legislators, and even to their country homes when the Legislature was not in session. In one session alone the bill for "supplies" amounted to $350,000.00, of which $150,000.00 was for the "refreshment room." Bills contracted to pander to the gross appetites of these "statesmen" were always promptly paid, while the unfortunate inmates of the lunatic asylum were suffering for want of proper food and clothing, the public schools were closed because the teachers could not be paid, and convicts were being pardoned from the penitentiary because they could not be fed. To have used all that was purchased, every member of the House and Senate must have used one gallon of whiskey per day, with a few extra bottles of ale and wine thrown in, and smoked not less than one dozen cigars within the same time.[77]

But the most gigantic of the frauds was the "Printing Ring" —the system by which the State Treasury was depleted more effectively than by any other. Again let the Fraud Reports tell the story. Whilst fraud, bribery and corruption were rife in every department of the State government, nothing has equalled the magnitude and infamy attending the management of public printing. While its "ring-leaders" were State officials, members of the General Assembly who were not actually in the ring themselves sold their votes to it for the highest prices. In that way the "Printing Ring" covered a more extended sphere of influence, and embraced a greater number of different classes of people than any of the others—the partisan press and party leaders throughout the State—judges, lawyers, editors, reporters and lobbyists, male and female, white and black.

Under the State printer system, whenever the conspirators wanted to get through a very large appropriation, they simply made the figures even larger, so that the total amount appropriated would include the bribes necessary to secure the majority for its passage. In this way the enormous sum of $98,000.00 was paid for the passage of a single printing bill. "The testimony against the conspirators was sufficient, in any court, to consign almost every one of them to the penitentiary for life." In this particular enterprise there was the anomaly of "a ring within a ring." Josephus Woodruff, white, Clerk of the Senate, and A. O. Jones, a northern mulatto, Clerk of the House, organized what was known as the Republican Printing Company, a close corporation, of which they were the sole members. When, in their official capacity, these worthies advertised for certain printing contracts, they would award the contracts to themselves. Their jobs giving Woodruff and Jones favorable position on the inside, they were finally able to drive the Carolina Printing Company, their only competitor, which had been originally organized by Scott, Chamberlain and

---

[77]Fraud Report, pp. 8-13, 170, 812.

others, into liquidation and thus secure to themselves the entire field.[78]

The ingenuity with which new schemes for public plunder were constantly devised was amazing. Even the enumeration of the schemes would pall upon the senses of the reader. Of those not already mentioned, some of the more notorious were the ones connected with the Sinking Fund; with the issue of fraudulent legislative pay certificates; with the furnishing of the State House; and with the management of the State penitentiary.

In every department of the State government the grasping hand of the plunderer was seen. The miscreants stole even from the unfortunate lunatics in the State asylum, using the money to supply themselves with expensive cigars and brandy that cost twenty dollars a gallon. Dr. J. F. Ensor, the superintendent of the asylum, who was an honest Republican, was told when he applied for the money which had been appropriated for the support of his institution, that the State Treasury was empty. Funds to conduct the institution for a time had to be raised on the personal notes of three of the State officials and certain merchants of Columbia and Charleston extended special accommodations to the superintendent in order to keep the unfortunate inmates of the institution from being turned out into the street.[79]

The free school system was a farce. The County School Commissioners (County Superintendents of Education, as they are now termed) presented a sad picture—dishonest and ignorant, some of them could not read or write. The schools had no funds. Of the $300,000.00 appropriated for them at the legislative session of 1871-72, there was not one dollar with which to pay the teachers. The negroes were better off as to educational advantages than the whites, for they received some assistance from benevolent people at the North. "The school sessions were irregular, the teachers became discouraged, the white taxpayers were naturally disgusted, and the entire system had sunk into a state of disrepute and worthlessness." [80]

The Rev. B. F. Whittemore, of Massachusetts, commonly known as "Parson" Whittemore, was a typical carpetbag leader,

[78]Fraud Reports, pp. 217, 251, etc.
[79]Reynolds, p. 220.
[80]Ibid., 134, 219.

and was one of the most picturesque characters connected with the Reconstruction period. He probably held the negro more completely under the sway of his personality than any man who ever lived in South Carolina. Whittemore was a man of force and determination, and he possessed considerable personal magnetism. He was a large man, with fine physique and a striking face, to which strength was added by a long flowing beard, which caused him to resemble the most venerable of the patriarchs. In speaking, his enunciation was clear and distinct, and his mellifluous tones had a carrying power which enabled him to be heard throughout the largest assemblages, even when speaking in conversational tones. It is said that Whittemore's power over the negroes was largely due to the fact that he sang so well at meetings, whether religious or political, that his appearance was always hailed joyously by the dusky crowds which flocked to hear him.[81]

When Whittemore first appeared on the political horizon in South Carolina, the Freedmen's Bureau had just promulgated the rule that all negroes whose marriages in slavery time were only mutual agreements were required to have their marriages confirmed by a minister. "This injunction as to remarriage was scrupulously obeyed and preachers made large sums of money which were frequently extorted from old, poor or ignorant negroes, who had grandchildren and great-grandchildren.[82] Whittemore, being a minister of the northern Methodist Church, established a fixed fee of two dollars for each marriage performed, with the result that the negroes flocked to him in such numbers that he soon amassed a competency.

Whittemore was elected to Congress from the First Congressional District, which included Darlington, where he resided. In 1870 he was detected in having sold cadetships to West Point and Annapolis, and he was expelled from Congress. Whittemore admitted that he had received from a New York broker two thousand dollars in cash for the right to name a cadet to West Point, but claimed that he had devoted the money to political and educational purposes. This incident made him notorious throughout the United States as the Congressman who trafficked in cadetships. The "Parson" appealed to his dusky constituents for vindication, and they enthusiastically

---

[81]Ku Klux Report (minority), p. 441; Fleming, Nos. 6 and 7, p. 4.
[82]Reynolds, p. 133.

gave it to him by re-electing him to Congress by an immense majority. On a motion, however, of General John A. Logan, of Illinois, which was adopted by a vote of 131 to 24, Congress refused to re-admit Whittemore, on the ground that he was "a man of infamous character."

Whittemore returned home, and, in the fall which followed his repudiation by Congress, was elected State Senator from Darlington. While in this position he became one of the most conspicuous of the State's plunderers. Josephus Woodruff kept a diary, and in it appears this entry: "Wednesday, Jan. 15, 1873. Collected certificate for $945.00 and paid for Whittemore's watch. Gracious Goodness! Whittemore will have received somewhere about $10,000 this session! That ought to satisfy him! He is always, though, after more!"

When the Democrats came into power in 1877, Whittemore was still a State Senator from Darlington. Finding that the Democratic Committee on Frauds was hot on his trail, he applied for, and received, leave of absence to visit "a sick family" in Massachusetts. *Pairing with a member of the Investigating Committee in the Senate,* he took the train and was not seen or heard from afterwards.[83]

---

[83]James A. Leland's A Voice from South Carolina, p. 228.

CHAPTER VIII

THE CONSTABULARY AND THE MILITIA

One of the matters that first engaged the attention of the carpetbag-negro leaders was the organization of the police and the militia of the State. Under the plan adopted the police consisted of a Chief Constable for the State at large, a deputy chief constable for each county, and under each deputy chief as many deputy constables as conditions in a county might require. As an aid to the constabulary, an armed force of one hundred men, called the State Guard, twenty of whom were mounted, was organized.

An elaborate system was provided for the militia, which was known as the National Guard of South Carolina, and heavy penalties were imposed upon any armed bodies other than militia for "organizing, drilling or parading." The militia was composed of negro troops. The whites were not allowed to form militia companies.

But there was no intention of depending entirely upon the militia, the constabulary or the "armed force" for the perpetuation of carpetbag and negro rule. A joint resolution was passed by the Legislature as soon as it assembled for the first time, requesting the Governor to take such action as may be necessary to have the more important towns in the State garrisoned by United States troops, that peace and order may be preserved and the rights of the people of the State protected. Thus the marauders who were looting the treasury admitted from the beginning their inability to continue their nefarious work unless they had Federal bayonets at their back. Their rule in South Carolina was characterized throughout by appeals of this nature to the national government, which was prompt to respond.

Scott appointed as chief of the constabulary—the "strong-arm squad"—John E. Hubbard of New York, a man of the most unsavory reputation, who could be depended upon to do whatever underhanded and brutal jobs were necessary to terrorize the whites. The class of thugs with whom Hubbard surrounded himself became equally notorious in the State. Scott also imported James E. Kerrigan, a New York gunman, and a picked body of gangsters to protect himself and his friends and kill off their enemies.[84]

The constables were armed with Winchester repeating rifles, as well as with pistols. There were about as many negroes as whites on the force, and they were all ruffians from the lowest classes of both races, always ready to contribute to a row, and quick to kill when one was started. The primary purpose of the authorities in keeping bodies of such desperate men under arms was to exasperate the white people beyond endurance, and thus bring about disturbances which would insure the continuance of the United States troops in support of the Republican party in the State.

But Scott, who from the time of his inauguration was laying plans for his re-election, early set about, with the aid of Adjutant and Inspector General Moses, enrolling and arming a very large militia force, to be used, together with the constabulary, in carrying the election.

Before the campaign commenced, Scott made a speech in Washington in which he advertised to the world that "the only law for these people [South Carolinians] was the Winchester rifle"; and when he returned to South Carolina, he put this idea into execution by further increasing his negro militia and supplying them with arms and an abundance of ammunition. As the time for the election approached, Scott secured from the War Department ten thousand of the newly perfected Springfield rifles (thus anticipating without any authority of law, the State's quota of arms from the general government for twenty years), and placed fourteen regiments of the negro militia on full war footing. No concealment was made of the fact that this was for the purpose of carrying the election. When election day came, there were ninety-six thousand negroes enrolled in the militia, practically all the negro voters in the State.

Before the arming of the negroes there was very little lawlessness—after that, the militia caused considerable increase in crime.

The comment of the Congressional Investigating Committee on the militia situation was that "The design of the [militia] law itself will be best exhibited by the improper use made of it during the summer of the next year after its passage, which,

[84]Reynolds, p. 152.

as contemplated in its enactment, was made to contol the election of that year, the Governor himself being a candidate for re-election." [85]

The Republican Convention was held on July 26, 1870, and Scott was renominated for Governor, and Chamberlain for Attorney-General. A. J. Ransier, a negro day laborer from Charleston, was nominated for Lieutenant Governor. Ransier was a man of little education and was especially offensive—sometimes insolent — in his demands for "equal rights" — meaning thereby social equality. The white people of the State had become so aroused at what had taken place that they had determined to do their utmost to wrest the government from the hands of the spoilers. A convention of Conservatives (Democrats) and Republicans of the better class was held in Columbia on June 15, 1870, and a new political organization was effected, known as the "Union Reform Party of South Carolina." R. B. Carpenter, a New Englander, reared in Kentucky, who was judge of the circuit in which Charleston was situated, then regarded as among the ablest and most available of the Republicans in the State, was nominated for Governor by the new party, while M. C. Butler, who had been a distinguished cavalry leader in the Confederate army, was nominated for Lieutenant Governor.

The Conservatives made a strenuous fight, but to no avail. The carpetbaggers and scalawags had so estranged the negroes from the respectable white people (the negroes' best friends) that the effort to convert them to the reform ticket failed. Besides, in addition to using the militia and constabulary, the

---

[85]See the testimony of F. J. Moses, Chief Constable Hubbard, the gunman Kerrigan, and other Republicans, given the Democratic Legislative Investigating Committee, and published in the Fraud Reports.

"Governor Scott would order me to send men to any county where the Republican party most needed encouragement and reorganization. The deputies were authorized and instructed to attend all political meetings, and report the political condition of the county to me, and I would report the same to the Governor."—From testimony of Chief Constable Hubbard before the Democratic Legislative Investigating Committee. "We can carry the county if we get constables enough, by encouraging the militia and frightening the poor white man [i.e., the poorer class of whites]. I am going into the campaign for Scott."—From letter of J. W. Anderson, Deputy Constable of York County, to Chief Constable Hubbard, 1870. "We are going to have a hard time up here, and we must have more constables. I will carry the election here with the militia, if the constables will work with me. I am giving out ammunition all the time. Tell Scott he is all right here now."—From letter of Joe Crews, a notorious carpetbagger of Laurens, 1870.

Radicals had all the election machinery in their own hands. Fraud on the part of the Radicals was rampant.[86]

The militia and the constabulary, as was intended should be the case, had been much in evidence during the campaign. The militia made themselves very offensive to the white people. They moved about the country in companies or in squads, particularly at night, and in the rural districts sparsely settled by the whites, firing off their guns to the terror of women and children. They made the most trivial occasion the excuse for a drill or parade, and would generally choose for their manoeuvres some frequented thoroughfare, where they would march along in company front, and with bayonets fixed and flags flying so as to occupy the entire way, greatly to the annoyance of passers-by.[87]

The negroes, becoming daily more intolerable in their bearing, offered indignities of all kinds to the whites. Crime among them was frequent, and at the instigation of their evil leaders they passed to actual deeds of violence. The torch applied secretly in the night time was their favorite method of getting even with their enemies.

The conduct of the militia was particularly offensive in Union and Laurens counties. There were five companies in Laurens County under Lieutenant Colonel Joe Crews. They constantly paraded the streets in a riotous manner, as if inviting trouble, their evident intention being to annoy the white people who had to get out of the way for them.[88]

---

[86]"The reform movement of 1870 was practically an effort to correct the mistake [of the white people] in 1868. It recognized the evils of party lines drawn according to race and color, and aimed at reconciling the two races. * * * [However] the events from 1865 to 1870 had removed the two races in South Carolina very far apart politically, and, to bring them together again, the reformers had to cover more ground than time permitted."—W. L. Trenholm's Local Reform in South Carolina (pamphlet).

The Republicans "committed frauds in a dozen different ways"—some voted many times, and there were instances where even women and minors were permitted to vote.—Report of the Congressional Investigating Committee. "The election law of the State is one which could not be better calculated to produce frauds by affording the facilities to commit and conceal them, and, tempted by these facilities, we cannot doubt that in many instances they were committed." —Statement of Judge Poland of the Congressional Investigating Committee.

[87]Reynolds, p. 145.

[88]A. A. Taylor, a Republican negro, says in his work, The Negro in South Carolina During the Reconstruction (p. 190): "Unfortunately, too, the negro militia was not wisely handled. Under Joe Crews, the white Lieutenant Colonel, the militiamen did so much parading and unnecessary talking about how they intended to keep order, and they made so many arrests that the whites organized in opposition."

Crews met a violent end. He was assassinated from ambush, in 1875, while riding on the public highway. His slayer was never apprehended, and hence it is not known whether the killing was due to his political activities or to someone's desire for personal revenge. Crews, for reasons besides political, had made many enemies.

As a member of the Legislature, Joe Crews had started in early to rob the State and accept bribes. A native white man, he was always very bitter in his denunciation of the white people of the State. He had been a negro trader before the war and after it became a negro lover, associating with the other race on terms of social equality. He was a regular firebrand in Laurens County, where his bitter and incendiary speeches kept the community in such a constant state of excitement that it needed only a spark to set it aflame. He openly advised the negroes to use their guns on the whites, and told them that "matches were cheap."[89]

Many other radical leaders, both whites and negroes, inflamed the minds of the masses in political harangues by telling them not to yield anything to the white man, of whom they were the social equals in every respect; that they were backed by the State government, which, in turn, had back of it the army of the United States.

The whites were without organization, but they armed themselves as best they could, and prepared to defend themselves. When actual clashes occurred, the negroes generally got the worst of it, as their militia was without discipline and was very little more than an armed mob. The company commanders were usually ignorant negroes, some of whom, without any education whatever, had to sign their vouchers with a crossmark. The majority of them knew little or nothing about military drill, so that their efforts at "showing off" were ludicrous, though objectionable.

As the campaign progressed, the commanding influence of the Loyal League among the negroes became manifest. Having taken a hide-bound oath to support the Republican ticket, a negro who, under the influence of his white friends, tried to break away from it was visited with persecution by his race, which in many instances extended to personal violence. The feeling between the races grew very bitter, and it was feared that there would be serious riots on election day. Incipient riots occurred at Laurens, Yorkville (now York) and Charleston, but, owing to the moderation displayed by the leaders among the white people, who restrained the more turbulent of their race, so as to afford the Radicals no excuse for calling on the Federal troops, nothing of a very serious nature occurred.

[89]Leland, p. 55.

As was the case with every other governmental activity, money of the taxpayers was outrageously squandered upon the militia and constabulary. At least two-thirds of the enormous expense incurred in the enrollment of the militia was a fraud upon the State and for which no consideration was received except political services rendered the Governor. In this way employment was given to local leaders, who, while ostensibly organizing the militia, were, in reality, organizing the Republican party for the approaching campaign.

The State constabulary and the "armed force" were special pets of the administration, and were frequently permitted to render and collect accounts for fictitious services which had never been performed.

The Republican Legislative Investigating Committee in 1871-72 severely arraigned Scott's militia activities, saying that "in the enrollment and organization of the militia, as well as in the armed force employed by the Governor, there was a most ample and complete opportunity for ambitious political partisans and aspirants for re-election to arm and equip a force of personal friends and advocates and pay them * * * not out of their own purse, but 'out of any moneys in the treasury not otherwise appropriated.' " The committee further reported that the "cost of enrolling and arming the State militia was $374,696.59," in which transactions the committee declared that "a glaring robbery of the treasury for personal ambition and gain had probably been perpetrated." According to the committee, the total expense of the militia during Scott's first term, including the constabulary and the "armed force," was $421,159.25.[90] Scott came back at the Legislature by refusing to approve the appropriation for legislative expenses, alleging as a reason for his action that the amount originally put in the bill, and which, he said, was ample for the purposes, had been fraudulently changed from $125,000 to $265,000.

---

[90]A contract was made for changing the rifles of the State government from muzzle-loaders to breech-loaders at a certain price per rifle. Moses, at the time Adjutant and Inspector General, and later Governor, added for himself a bonus of one dollar for each rifle remodeled. The bonus netted Moses ten thousand dollars and was paid out of the public treasury. See Moses' testimony before the Democratic Legislative Investigating Committee.

After Scott's re-election the mad orgies in government continued with renewed vigor. Things went from bad to worse. Deeds of violence on the part of both races became everyday affairs, and the State government seeming powerless to prevent them, it looked as if utter chaos would ensue. Scott called for more Federal troops. He was promised by President Grant all the military aid he needed, and very soon afterwards the number of Federal troops in the State was greatly increased.

CHAPTER IX

THE KU KLUX

"Crimes among the negroes—murder, arson, burglary—became so frequent [in the South] that the whites were compelled to form a secret order for their protection."[91]   In South Carolina the arrogance of the negro militia and the menace of the negro secret societies became so great that the people in certain sections of the State banded themselves together for self-protection in the famous organization known as the Ku Klux Klan.   The order existed in the South as early as 1865, but the period immediately following the end of the military government (1868) marked its greatest activity.   It disbanded about 1871.

The spread of the Ku Klux through the South may be said to have been due primarily to the fact that it found a fertile field for growth in the generally demoralized condition of things which followed the War—serious lawlessness among certain classes of the whites, turbulence on the part of the negroes, and the fear that the negroes would break out in a general uprising.   The Ku Klux Klan seemed to meet a need which the State governments failed to supply—in fact, there was no State government, nor anything worthy of the name—only the corrupt and tyrannical rule of aliens, renegades and negroes, whose opportunity for looting the public treasury was rendered possible by the power of Federal bayonets.

As has been shown, conditions in South Carolina were particularly bad.   The civil courts were entirely inadequate. Many of the judges were venal, and the juries, made up almost entirely of negroes, were easily and shamelessly bribed.   Most of those convicted were pardoned by the Executive, whose reckless and flagrant use of the power made a travesty of justice.   Governor Scott released no less than six hundred convicts during his four years of office.

The election machinery was all in the hands of the carpetbaggers and negroes, and the election laws which they passed were especially framed so as to admit of fraud ; the constabulary and the negro militia aided in carrying the elections for the

---

[91]The Encyclopædia Britannica (Eleventh Edition), Vol. 25, p. 504.

Republicans, and in other ways made themselves very objectionable. The deplorable condition of the State arose from the Reconstruction Acts, which the people of the South believed to be unconstitutional and which could only be sustained by force of arms.[92] Specifically the Ku Klux Klan owed its spread throughout the State to its use as an offset to the Freedmen's Bureau and the Bureau's despised offspring, the Loyal League, which were constantly stirring up strife between the races and everlastingly advocating equal rights. The Ku Klux Klan is said to have existed in South Carolina as early as 1868. It did not figure to a great extent, however, until the latter part of 1870, and it would not have become very active then but for Scott's policy of arming the negroes through his militia organizations, and of refusing to permit the whites to form militia companies. After the election in 1870, the militia became more intolerant and insolent than ever and the whites armed themselves for self-protection. In every community where the Klan became active, the cause was due to the negroes having committed murder, arson, or other serious crime.[93]

The original purpose of the Ku Klux Klan was simply to frighten the negroes into good behavior by playing upon their superstitious fears, and some of the best men in South Carolina were originally numbered among its members. However, intended at first for self-protection only, abuses in the organization arose later; so that it soon lost its original significance, and the members took to unwarrantable acts—whipping and banishing the more insolent negroes and the more troublesome carpetbaggers and scalawags. Most of the better class then left the organization, and the more restless and lawless obtained control of it. "Outlaws found that the name and disguise of the order afforded them protection and their crimes [even murder] were committed in its name."[94]

In January, 1871, a harmless and helpless white man, who had lost an arm in the Confederate army, was brutally murdered by forty negro militiamen on a highway near the town of

---

[92]"No one who was not a citizen of the South in those days could appreciate the situation that gave rise to the Ku Klux. Something outside the law was needed to keep in check the Republican administration and its ignorant followers, upheld by the power of Grant's administration."—Davis' manuscript.
[93]Reynolds, p. 182.
[94]Fleming, No. 3, p. 5.

Union. The Sheriff of the county arrested thirteen of the negroes and placed them in jail. Two of his posse were badly wounded in the effort to make the arrest. The Ku Klux Klan took two of the prisoners from the jail and shot them to death. Three of the prisoners escaped, and the remaining eight were about to be removed to Columbia by order of the Court, when members of the Klan, numbering some one thousand to fifteen hundred, all mounted and disguised, took them from the jail and shot them to death. "This bloody work was done quietly. There was no uproar. * * * The mounted men retired as quietly as they had come, their ranks well kept and their movements marked by a precision which was well-nigh military."[95]

The terrible affair created a profound sensation throughout the country. The Klan continued to operate in Union County, although with less bloody results. Their activities were also very marked in Spartanburg and York Counties. So serious had the trouble become in these three counties that law and order meetings were held by the conservative class of white people urging a cessation of deeds of violence. The gravity of the situation, and the fact that his re-election had been accomplished, moved Scott to endeavor to co-operate with the conservative element of the whites in their efforts for peace. He disbanded his militia in the riotous counties, and, in several instances, he removed incompetent officials, and appointed good men in their places. This show of decency on his part had its effect. With the negro militia in the troubled sections disbanded, the Ku Klux became inactive by the early part of 1871, and the order went out of existence a short while afterwards.

Congress had passed (1870–71), what were known as the Enforcement Acts or "Force Bills." They were ostensibly directed against lawlessness in the South, but were really designed for the perpetuation of negro domination in that section.

Scott confessed his inability to cope with the situation in South Carolina, and appealed to President Grant for assistance. The President thereupon issued a proclamation, stating that "combinations of armed men, unauthorized by law, are now disturbing the peace and safety of the citizens of the State of South Carolina, and committing acts of violence in said State

[95]Reynolds, p. 185.

of a character and to an extent which render the powers of
the State and its offices inadequate to the task of protecting
life and property and restoring order there." The proclamation further declared that the Governor of South Carolina had
called on the President "for such part of the military force of
the United States as may be necessary and adequate to protect
said State and the citizens thereof against the domestic violence
hereinbefore mentioned." The proclamation concluded by
calling upon the unlawful assemblages mentioned to disperse
within twenty days.

A Joint Select Committee of Congress, partisan Republican
in politics and therefore in sympathy with the Reconstruction
governments, reported that many crimes, some of them of a
revolting nature, had been committed in the South, by whites
upon the negroes, for political reasons only. Congress then
passed (April 20, 1871), another "Force Bill," commonly
known as the Ku Klux Act, giving the United States Courts
jurisdiction in Ku Klux cases, and authorizing the President
to use the land and naval forces of the United States to sup-
press Ku Klux disorders, and to suspend the writ of habeas
corpus whenever he deemed it necessary.

Under the provisions of this Act President Grant declared
martial law and suspended the writ of habeas corpus in nine
counties of South Carolina—Spartanburg, York, Union,
Laurens, Chester, Newberry, Fairfield, Lancaster, Chesterfield.
These were the nine counties in which the result of the guberna-
torial election in 1870 had been most doubtful and where Scott's
negro militia had been correspondingly overbearing and lawless in carrying out the fixed policy of the Governor to secure
his re-election by force, if necessary.

The passage of the Ku Klux Act and the declaration of
martial law in certain counties of South Carolina, after quiet
had been restored to the State, were part and parcel of the
partisan course toward the South of President Grant and the
National Republican party then in control of all branches of the
United States government.

Large military forces were sent into the nine counties to
make arrests, which were effected by squads of United States
Cavalry, usually in the night time, without warrants, and often
without any evidence against the parties, other than the un-
corroborated statement of some ignorant and malicious negro,

or of some vindictive individual who sought this method of revenge for a private grievance. Several hundred persons were arrested in Spartanburg County, two hundred were arrested in Union, and one hundred and ninety-five in York, while the other six counties in which martial law had been declared were called upon to contribute their quota of victims. The jails of the State were soon filled with those who were suspected of being members of the Klan, and they were held in confinement for weeks and months before being tried or discharged. Arrests in York County were made on charges brought by one Isaac A. Postle (otherwise called Isaac, the Apostle), who, it was alleged, had been intimidated at the general election in 1872 on account of his "race, color and previous condition of servitude."[96]

In a message to Congress President Grant said that "notwithstanding the large number of persons [arrested], it is believed that no innocent person is now held in custody." It is unbecoming, to say the least, for the chief magistrate of the nation in a message to Congress, to judge guilty a man awaiting trial, and the fact that President Grant did so is indicative of the intense feeling then in the North against the South. As a matter of fact many of the persons arrested in South Carolina on Ku Klux charges were innocent as was shown by their subsequently being acquitted, or set free without trial by a hostile court.

The Ku Klux trials, which were held at the November (1871) term of the United States Court in Columbia, aroused the greatest interest throughout the State. Of the large number arrested, about fifty pled guilty, while only five of them were tried and convicted. The sentences imposed fines, or terms of imprisonment, or both, the fine ranging from fifty dollars to one thousand dollars, and the terms of imprisonment from one month to five years. Some of those who drew the longer terms were sent to the Albany penitentiary. There were other trials at the April (1872) term of the Federal Court in Charleston, when twenty-eight persons were convicted and sentenced, and still other trials at the November (1872) term of the United States Court in Columbia, when nine were convicted and sentenced.

[96]Reynolds, p. 208.

When it is remembered that the Federal Court was very hostile to the white people of South Carolina, and that its juries were tampered with and its witnesses suborned by the prosecutors, the fact that, of the large number of persons arrested upon Ku Klux charges, so few were convicted, one realizes the iniquity of these wholesale and indiscriminate arrests by the United States army.

Dr. J. Rufus Bratton, a highly respected citizen and a leading physician of Yorkville (now York), having reason to believe that his arrest on Ku Klux charges was sought and unwilling to trust his fate with a prejudiced court, left the country. He located in London, Province of Ontario, Canada, where he resumed the practice of his profession. In 1872, he was seized at night, blindfolded and gagged by agents of the United States Government, brought across the international boundary and, thence, brought back to Yorkville. Friends in Yorkville furnishing bond, he was released from actual custody to await trial. The Canadian Government, indignant at the violation of its rights—the trespass upon its territory and the taking therefrom of a person by force—demanded the immediate and full release of Dr. Bratton. The United States government promptly responded by setting him free.

It is stated on reliable authority that the Ku Klux Klan never operated in Laurens County. However, there had been a race riot there on the day after the election in 1870, precipitated by the gross misconduct of the negro militia, in which one of their number had been killed and two injured. As a result of this riot, and at the instance of the notorious Joe Crews, about forty citizens of Laurens County, some of them men of the very highest character and standing, were arrested early in 1872, by a body of United States soldiers, accompanied by John B. Hubbard as deputy United States Marshal. The specific charge preferred was conspiracy against the rights of persons of color, contrary to the Act of Congress of March 30, 1870, known as the Enforcement Act or "Force Bill." Those arrested were imprisoned for some time, first in Columbia and afterwards in Charleston, and were subjected to tyrannical and oppressive treatment. The Federal grand jury, sitting in Charleston, indicted all of them for conspiracy and murder. They were admitted to bail, but never tried. Think of it, men arrested nearly two years after the alleged offense

was said to have been committed, thrown in jail where they
were treated most brutally, and then not brought to trial for
want of sufficient evidence against them!

Among the Laurens prisoners was John A. Leland, Ph.D.,
a scholarly gentleman, nearly sixty years of age, who was a
ruling elder in the Presbyterian Church, and whose entire life
had been one of probity. Major Leland, at the time of his
arrest, was President of the Laurensville Female Academy.
The evidence upon which he was arrested was subsequently
shown to be of the flimsiest nature. In his book, *A Voice from
South Carolina*, he gives an interesting account of his arrest
and his jail experience. Describing his arrest, he writes: "I
merely bowed 'good morning' to my household * * * and
sallied forth, followed by my guard, with his piece at his
shoulder. Each window towards the gate was filled with the
heads of the young ladies of the college—witnessing this strange
exit of their president."[97] "We reached this [Columbia] Jail
about sunset on yesterday and were marched here from the
depot, some half mile, 'two and two,' Newgate fashion. The
procession was a gloomy one; thirty-six hungry and jaded men,
encumbered with all the baggage we had, and moving through
the middle of the street was a mob of negroes of all ages and
both sexes, cursing and jeering at us from both sidewalks."[98]

Major Leland and his fellow-prisoners were showered with
attentions from the people of Columbia—the best people socially, morally and intellectually.[99] The ladies of the community,
in particular, showed great kindness in visiting them, and in
supplying them with delicacies with which to supplement their
coarse prison fare. Among the most frequent of these visitors
was Mrs. James Woodrow, the aunt-in-law of Woodrow Wilson, and Mrs. George Howe, whose son married a sister of
the country's great President during the World War. Mrs.
Woodrow is still an honored resident of Columbia. Major
Leland's diary states that, on one occasion when he was permitted to attend Church and communion service in Columbia,
accompanied by a deputy sheriff, he "heard an excellent sermon
from Rev. Doctor Joseph R. Wilson" [the father of Woodrow
Wilson].

[97]P. 95.
[98]P. 99.
[99]P. 124.

To the credit of President Grant be it said that, in the summer of 1873, he pardoned all the Ku Klux prisoners who had been convicted, but who had not at that time served out their sentences. During the existence of the Klan it effectually curbed the offensive activities of Scott's negro militia, and sounded the death-knell of the Loyal League in South Carolina.[100]

After four years of the misrule of the carpetbagger and negro, they were so thoroughly entrenched in the State that it seemed as if it would be impossible to dispossess them. All the appeals of the taxpayers fell upon ears which were deaf to every moral sense, and minds which were completely permeated with graft and greed. Enmity to the white race, an insane desire for social equality, characterized every act of the evil men who were drunk with the power of public plunder. The miscreants were backed throughout by the civil and military authorities of the United States. President Grant, who had shown such generous feeling toward the Southern people during and just after the war, fell under the influence of the radical Republicans who had elevated him to the Presidency, and became an oppressor of the South. By reason of his high office he was able to do the Southern people much harm.

In the Atlantic Monthly for April, 1901, D. H. Chamberlain wrote:[101] "So ingrained was the disregard of Southern Democrats [by Northern Radicals] in all affairs of the State that concerned the political control of the South, so inflexible was the determination of officials and leaders at Washington to keep the heel on the neck. * * * To this tide of folly, and worse. President Grant constantly yielded."

---

[100]It is of interest to note that some years later the United States Supreme Court declared all the "Force Bills" of Reconstruction , times, including the "Ku Klux Act," to be unconstitutional in the main features used in oppressing the South. Unfortunately, however, this decision came too late to save the Southern people from the suffering that the United States Government inflicted upon them under the authority of the "Force Bills."
[101]P. 477.

CHAPTER X

"THE ROBBER GOVERNOR"

When the campaign of 1872 opened, the notorious F. J. Moses, Jr., was the leading candidate for the Republican nomination for Governor. Many of the Radical leaders, both white and negro, pretending to be shocked at so much corruption in the State government, had become loudly clamorous for reform, and were apparently anxious to defeat his nomination. Their efforts were unsuccessful, however, for when the Republican Convention met on August 21, Moses was nominated over three other candidates, one of whom was D. H. Chamberlain.[102]

R. H. Gleaves, a Northern negro residing in Beaufort, was nominated for Lieutenant Governor.

The opposition, still dissatisfied, bolted the nominations, and held a convention in Columbia on August 27, at which strenuous speeches were made in denunciation of Moses. Among the crimes openly charged against him was that, when speaker, he had issued fraudulent pay certificates to the amount of $1,200,000. The bolters' convention nominated for Governor, Reuben Tomlinson, a Northern Quaker who lived in Charleston, and for Lieutenant Governor, James N. Hayne, a Barnwell negro. The campaign was utterly lacking in interest. It was a contest of Republican factions, between whom there was little for the whites to choose. At least 30,000 voters did not go to the polls. Moses was elected by a vote of 69,838, as against 36,533 for Tomlinson.

The only way in which to account for Moses is on the theory that he was a degenerate—a theory which is abundantly justified by the circumstances of his life. He was a man of prepossessing appearance and excellent address. A member of a well-known and respected Southern family, he began life as a fire-eating secessionist. He was private secretary to Governor F. W. Pickens at the beginning of the War of Secession, and constantly made the boast that it was he "who tore down the American flag from Fort Sumter, and, treading it underfoot, hoisted the Confederate ensign in its place."

[102]Chamberlain held no public office during Moses' administration.

Moses was one of the few whites, known as "scalawags," who joined the carpetbaggers when they infested the State and allied themselves with the negroes to form the Republican party. In the scramble for office which ensued among the spoilers, he outdistanced most of the others, for he drew two offices and filled them concurrently — one executive and the other legislative—Adjutant and Inspector General and Speaker of the House of Representatives. In both positions Moses displayed exceptional qualifications as a public plunderer, and, when the Republican party in South Carolina nominated him for Governor, it sounded the lowest depths of its degradation. Moses was absolutely lost to every moral sense, and was decidedly the worst Governor the State has ever had; so much so that he has gone down in history as the "Robber Governor," His shameful notoriety soon spread throughout the Union. He led a grossly immoral and profligate life and dissipated money as fast as he could get hold of it. Coming into the office of Governor without a dollar in the world, he, nevertheless, judging from the scale on which he lived, must have spent between $30,000 and $40,000 a year, while his salary was only $3,500.

Moses did not reside at the Executive Mansion, but rented it out, and bought for his use as a residence while Governor the famous Preston Mansion (now Chicora College), for which he paid $40,000. This mansion, long the property of General Hampton's grandfather, was not only the finest residence in Columbia at that time, but was one of the finest in the entire South, while the grounds surrounding it were exceedingly beautiful. Moses fitted up the house and grounds in handsome style and lived in what, for those days, was regal splendor. His carriage and horses were the finest to be had. His expenditures otherwise were so large that when he went into voluntary bankruptcy at the expiration of his term, his assets were only $67,000, as against liabilities of more than $225,000.

Besides his other forms of dishonesty, Moses was the most accomplished bribe taker in the State's history, his career in this respect while Speaker and afterwards while Governor, being absolutely shameless. He sold everything connected with the Governor's duties which could be exchanged for money — honors, emoluments, pardons, and even empty military titles. The people of the State were aghast at Scott's pardon record, but Moses easily outdistanced it. Moses released 457 convicts during his two years of office—forty-one of them in a single month—a record which brought forth from the redoubtable Judge Mackey the remark that "the Executive Mansion throws a shadow broad and deep across the threshold of this court!"

While he was Governor, Moses was jointly indicted with J. L. Humbert, County Treasurer of Orangeburg, on a charge of conspiracy to rob the State. A bench warrant was issued for Moses, but as he refused to be arrested and called out three companies of negro militia, who guarded him at his office and at his residence for two days, no further steps were taken to arrest him. Chamberlain, who was one of the attorneys for Moses, made a motion in court to quash the indictment against him on the ground that a Governor could be reached only by impeachment proceedings. The motion was granted and the whole matter ended there, although there was no question as to the guilt of both Moses and Humbert.

Moses later acknowledged that he received $15,000 for approving, while Governor, a large printing bill of the Republican Printing Company, and that he used this money as the first payment on the purchase of the Preston mansion.[103]

Other officials were not behind Moses in corruption, for there was bribery and stealing everywhere. Seats in Congress were bought and sold. The courts and juries, the latter composed mainly of negroes, were so venal that there was no safety for life or property. Of the 124 members of the Legislature during Moses's administration, forty-nine were afterward conclusively proven to have been bribed, by their own endorsement of checks which they received. Republican leaders, who were poor men as a rule, defiantly flaunted their crimes before the public in the shape of fine raiment, costly furniture and dashing equipages. "There was a perfect pandemonium of profligacy —vice and dissipation were rampant."

The carpetbaggers and negroes were by this time in complete control, and the State was indeed prostrate. The New Englander, Pike, graphically sums up the condition in his *Prostrate State*. "The last administration [Scott's] stole right hand and left with a recklessness and audacity without parallel. * * * The whole of the late administration was a mass of rot-

---

[103]Moses' testimony before the Democratic Legislative Investigating Committee.

tenness, and the present administration [Moses'] is born of the corruption of that. * * * They plunder and they glory in it. They steal and defy you to prove it. * * * The Treasury of South Carolina has been so thoroughly gutted by the thieves * * * there is nothing left to steal. The note of any negro in the State is worth as much on the market as a South Carolina bond. It would puzzle even a Yankee carpetbagger to make anything out of the office of State Treasurer under such circumstances." [104]

Pike says of the State officials: "In the executive government, to be sure, the Governor [Moses] is white; he got his place by dancing at negro balls and speculating in negro delegates. But the Lieutenant Governor is colored, * * * and the Treasurer of the State, and nearly all the rest of the officials. Here was Columbia! Half the population was white, but the Senator was colored, and its representatives in the Legislature and the city government were nearly all colored men."

Pike's pen picture of the Legislature during Moses' term, whose sessions he witnessed, is an interesting study in black and white: "They were of every hue, from the light octoroon to the deep black. * * * The body was almost literally a black parliament, and it is the only one on the face of the earth which is the representative of a white constituency, and the professed exponent of an advanced modern civilization. * * * The Speaker is black, the clerk is black, the door-keepers are black, the little pages are black, the Chairman of the Ways and Means Committee is black, the chaplain is coal black."

The New England abolitionist evidently found the South Carolina Legislature entertaining. He says: "One of the first things that strikes a casual observer in this negro assembly is the fluency of debate—if the endless chatter that goes on can be dignified with this term. * * * He [negro legislator] is notoriously fond of a joke or an anecdote, and will burst into a loud guffaw on the smallest provocation. * * * This is considered a capital joke and a guffaw follows. The laugh goes round and then the peanuts are cracked and munched faster than ever; one hand being employed in fortifying the inner man with this nutriment of universal use, while the other enforces the views of the orator." [105]

---

[104] Pp. 26, 35, 38.
[105] Pp. 17, 28, 45.

A good idea of many of the legislative debates may be found in the following account of one which took place in the House of Representatives in 1873, the question under consideration being a proposed appropriation for the State penitentiary:

Minort (negro): "The appropriation is not a bit too large."

Humbert (negro): "The institution ought to be self-sustaining. The member only wants a grab at the money."

Hurley (white): "Mr. Speaker: True—" Humbert (to Hurley) "You shet you myuf, sah!" (Roars of laughter.)

Greene (negro): "That thief from Darlington (Humbert)— Humbert: "If I have robbed anything, I expect to be Ku-Kluxed by just such highway robbers as the member from Beaufort" (Greene).

Greene: "If the Governor (Moses) were not such a coward, he would have cowhided you before this, or got somebody else to do it."

Hurley: "If the gentleman from Beaufort (Greene) would allow the weapon named to be sliced from his cuticle, I might submit to the castigation."[106]

The negroes reveled in the luxury which surrounded them in the legislative halls and committee rooms, and were loathe to return to the hovels and shacks in which most of them lived. They did not hesitate, therefore, to resort to all sorts of expedients for stringing out the legislative session indefinitely at the expense of the taxpayers. The demand for the call of the aye's and no's, for instance, was carried to such an extreme that it became ridiculous to the spectator, but most costly to the State. Much time was also taken up with measures of no importance whatsoever, such as the chartering of negro societies with high-sounding titles: Young Men's Africanus Debating Club of Charleston; The Young Men's Free Enterprise Council of Georgetown; The American Union Literary Club of Gadsden. Richland County; the Union Republican Wide Awake Association of Charleston; the Ladies and Gentlemen of Charity Society of Lady Island; the Sons' and Daughters' Cain Manuel Society of Charleston.

This was the Legislature that in 1872 elected John J. Patterson United States Senator from South Carolina. It was afterward proved that Patterson bought the votes of the members

[106]From Leigh's Ten Years on a Georgia Plantation, p. 290, quoted in Rhodes's History of the United States, Vol. VII, p. 155.

of the Legislature in order to secure his election.[107] He said himself that the election cost him $40,000.

Patterson was afterward indicted and bound over for trial on a charge of bribery in the Senatorial election. As Patterson's condition was now one "when a fellow needs a friend," Moses removed the jury commissioner of Richland County and appointed John B. Dennis[108] to that position. According to the sworn statement which Dennis afterward made in regard to the matter, he undertook to manage the jury box in such a way as to insure Patterson's protection. "I would not," he said, "when listing the jury for the year, have or allow any name to go in the box that I thought to be in any way inimical to Patterson." The case against Patterson was finally dropped. A protest against his being seated was made to the United States Senate, but it went unheeded on the ground that it was unofficial and irregular, and John J. Patterson became the successor of John C. Calhoun.

From the beginning to the end of carpetbag rule the doctrine which was advocated with the greatest persistency was that of social equality. To attain that end was the height of the negro's ambition, and his white leaders, who backed him up in it, practiced what they preached. Reynolds says that "Most of the white Republicans ate and drank, walked and rode, went to public places, and ostensibly affiliated with negroes. * * * A prominent white Republican, rather priding himself on his education and refinement, once selected a negro clergyman to perform the funeral services over the dead body of his own child."[109]

Between 1868 and 1875 the negro Legislatures passed several civil rights acts whose purpose was to enforce equal rights for both races in matters of public accommodation and entertainment, as on railroads and in hotels, restaurants and theatres. The white people of the State were willing to acquiesce in the political and civil rights granted the negroes by the amendments to the Constitution of the United States, but were unwilling to

---

[107]Fraud Report, pp. 9, 10.
[108]Dennis was superintendent of the State penitentiary from 1873 to 1875. Both in the conduct of that institution and in various other activities in which he became involved from time to time, he was known as a ringleader among the plunderers.
[109]P. 501. The prominent white Republican here referred to is Chamberlain.

allow them, and never did allow them, entirely, equal social rights, even in cases required by State laws.[110]

The first attempt to apply the doctrine of equal social rights to the public institutions of the State was made, in Scott's administration, with the State Lunatic Asylum. The board of regents, composed of whites and negroes, sought to have an assistant physician of the institution, who was a negro, treat the white as well as the negro patients. Fortunately they were defeated in their nefarious undertaking by Dr. J. F. Ensor, the superintendent, a Republican, but a good man, whose service in the Federal army had been creditable, and whose administration of the affairs of the State Asylum had won for him the respect and good will of everyone in the State.

The assault upon the Institution for the Deaf and Dumb and the Blind, at Cedar Springs, Spartanburg County, was also unsuccessful, but at the expense of the institution itself. An order was issued that negro pupils should be admitted into the institution and that "such pupils when admitted must be domiciled in the same building, must eat at the same table, must be taught in the same classrooms and by the same teachers, and must receive the same attention, care and consideration as white pupils." The officials of the institution immediately resigned, and as none could be found to take their places, the institution remained closed for three years. In this way many unfortunate children who needed it were denied the benefit of this school.

But the University of South Carolina which had been for nearly three-quarters of a century one of the chief sources of pride to the people of the State, fell victim to the mania for social equality. Although the establishment of Claflin University at Orangeburg as a State college for negro students had made such a course inexcusable even from the standpoint that it was necessary, the board of trustees of the State University, half white and half negro, acting under the provisions of the carpetbagger constitution that all State-supported colleges and schools should be open to both races, determined, in 1873, to admit negroes to the State University. The first negro to be

[110]A. A. Taylor, the negro author, says, in his The Negro in South Carolina During Reconstruction, p. 160: "Because of the intense feeling existing between the races, social intercourse was impractical. The negroes early enacted a civil rights bill by which they hoped to break down the social barriers in restaurants, hotels and places of amusement, but the white men usually found some way to evade the law."

admitted was Henry E. Hayne, the Secretary of State, who matriculated in the law department. The members of the faculty who had not already been removed by the trustees resigned, and the student body, except the sons of carpetbaggers and scalawags, left the sacred walls.

Negro students then entered the University in considerable numbers. As they were unfitted to take collegiate courses, the curriculum was lowered to the standard of a high school. The once glorious institution continued thus prostituted until 1877, when the Democratic Legislature temporarily closed its doors.[111]

Governor Moses, in a message to the Legislature, deplored the closing of the institution for the Deaf and Dumb and the Blind, but insisted that it was only just that negro children should be admitted to the institution on terms of full social equality with the whites. He expressed regret that members of the University faculty had resigned on account of the matriculation of "the Hon. Henry E. Hayne, our colored Secretary of State, whom all who know him accord to be a true gentleman of the highest character and the strictest integrity."[112] Moses further characterized the University as "the healthy child of the present administration"; expressed the hope that "the narrow spirit of bigotry and prejudice had been banished from its portals"; and congratulated the State upon the fact that one of the professors at the University was a negro—and added that "this onward stride in the march of civilization was the harbinger of the happy day which is coming, when all class distinctions should be forever laid in the dust of the past."

Chamberlain, who was a member of the board of trustees at the time, approved of the turning over of the State University to the negroes. Later, when Governor, he declared in a message to the Legislature: "I do not hesitate to say that I think the University is now doing a good work, and deserves the support of the State."

---

[111]While the negroes controlled the State University, the young white men of the State who sought a collegiate education attended the denominational colleges within the State, or, else, institutions of learning outside the State. Some of these young men were so fortunate as to secure scholarships in Northern colleges. In this way there were no less than forty South Carolinians at Union College, Schenectady, New York, in 1876, the writer one of the number.

[112]Hayne was afterwards incriminated in some of the public stealing that disgraced the period.

CHAPTER XI

THE RIFLE CLUBS—THE TAXPAYERS' APPEAL TO GRANT

There had been for many years among the people in the South of German extraction social organizations known as "Schuetzen Vereins" ("shooting clubs"), for target shooting, picnics, dances, and other amusements. The purpose of these clubs was so manifestly peaceful that the carpetbagger government offered no opposition to them. When Scott inaugurated his policy of confining the State militia to the negroes and debarring the whites from sharing in the public arms, the white people began organizing "rifle clubs" modeled after the plan of the German "shooting clubs."

The first rifle club formed in South Carolina was the Carolina Rifle Club of Charleston, which was organized on July 30, 1869. Owing to the large and very turbulent negro population in Charleston—longshoremen and others of that class— riots and labor strikes began there early in the days of Reconstruction; and with all police authority—national, state, and municipal—arrayed on the side of the negroes against the whites, it soon became manifest that the whites "would be compelled to fall back upon the ultimate right of self defense by creating a volunteer police force of their own"—hence, the Carolina Rifle Club.

The constitution of the rifle club declared the purpose of the club to be "the promotion of social intercourse, and the enjoyment of its members by means of target shooting and such other amusements as they may determine." The club bought its own arms and equipment and paid its own expenses. No military titles were used; the Captain was known as the President, and the Lieutenants were known as Vice-Presidents, the Sergeants as Wardens, and the Corporals as Directors. The minutes of the organization referred only to shooting matches, parades, dinners, and other social functions, "no record being kept of the drills, nor of the fact that the members were held ready for their real object—the protection of their homes and families in the event of a riot."[113]

---

[113]This account of the origin of the rifle clubs is from General C. I. Walker's interesting pamphlet, The Carolina Rifle Club, pp. 15-21. General Walker was Captain of the Carolina Rifle Club during Reconstruction.

The Carolina Rifle Club was the basis for the other clubs formed in the city of Charleston, of which there became no less than ten by 1876. The movement spread during the administrations of Scott and Moses to other towns, and finally, during the administration of Chamberlain, it spread to the rural communities. The rural organizations were usually known as "sabre clubs" and were mounted. The sabre clubs were the forerunners of the Red Shirt organizations, which, in 1876, ousted the carpetbagger and elected Wade Hampton Governor of the State.

Since all military organizations not part of the State militia were prohibited by law, the rifle clubs had no legal status, but existed merely on sufferance. Indeed, Radical leaders were not averse to using them as a protection against their own negro militia.[114]

In a municipal election in Charleston riotous negroes took control of the city to such an extent that the Republican authorities were compelled to call on the Carolina Rifle Club for assistance in maintaining the law, and that organization, responding promptly, assembled at its armory and remained under arms all during the day.

On the day of the election in 1874, a near riot occurred in the streets of Columbia between the rival factions of Beverly Nash and Charles Minort, negro candidates for the State Senate from Richland County, and both corrupt. Minort was the colonel of the militia regiment to which the Columbia companies belonged, and, in advocacy of their leader, the militiamen, who were called out in uniform and under arms, acted in such an unseemly manner on election day that the peace of the community was seriously threatened. Immense crowds of both factions paraded up and down the streets, many of them intoxicated, and all of them beside themselves with election excitement. A considerable number were kept together in different parts of the city, ready to attack each other and bring on a bloody affray. The militia proceeded to the Governor's residence, and made such a boisterous demonstration that he, not knowing where else to turn for help, called on the officers of

---

[114]Chamberlain, in his address at the Fort Moultrie Centennial in Charleston in 1876, referred in complimentary terms to the rifle clubs present as a part of the "citizen soldiery" of the State.

the Richland Rifle Club, to know whether they would assist in preserving peace and order[114a] The officers of the club, deciding promptly to go to the aid of the distressed Governor, the President of the club, afterwards a Democratic Governor of South Carolina, replied to Moses, as follows:

> Office, Richland Rifle Club,
> Columbia, Oct. 5th, 1874.
>
> To his Excellency, F. J. Moses, Jr.,
> Governor of South Carolina.
> Sir:
> In response to your application made this afternoon to some of the officers of the Richland Rifle Club to obey an order of your Excellency to be ready as a posse comitatus to preserve the peace in case of a riot between the Minort and the Nash factions which your Excellency apprehends may occur to-night, as President of the Club, and after full consultation with its officers, I have the honor to inform you that the members of the Club are ready to discharge their duty as good citizens, and that they will promptly obey any written order to conserve the peace that your Excellency may extend.
> Very respectfully,
> Your o'b't serv't,
> Hugh S. Thompson,
> President.

In an almost incredibly short time seventy well disciplined and well drilled white soldiers, members of the Richland Rifle Club, had assembled. The knowledge that the rifle club was under arms had a wholesome effect upon the riotous negro militia. Governor Moses particularly thanked the Richland Rifle Club after quiet had been restored.[115]

Meanwhile a second Taxpayers' Convention had been held in Columbia, early in the year 1874. A resolution was adopted to the effect that taxation in the State had reached the last point of endurance; and that the taxpayers could not continue to bear the excessive burdens which were imposed upon them. The convention also prepared a memorial to Congress, which set forth that a majority of the members of the legislature owned no part whatsoever of the property taxed, while the minority owned so little that their pay as members was more than their entire interest as property holders. As a result of this condition of affairs the property owners had no voice in the government, while those imposing the taxes had no part of the burdens to bear. "The history of the country teaches," recited the memorial, "that taxation without representation is

---

[114a]The Richland Rifle Club had bought their arms from an official of the State government.
[115]New York *Herald*, October 6, 1876

tyranny." Attention was called to the following facts, among others: The public debt had increased during the six years of Republican rule from five million dollars to fifteen million, without one dollar in the way of results to show for it. Vast frauds had, in many other ways, been perpetrated upon the State.[116] Since corruption extended from the highest officials to the lowest and since the Governor controlled the avenues of justice, it was impossible to detect and punish these crimes. In fact, the entire system was one of self-sustaining and self-protecting corruption, for the elections were conducted by persons appointed in the interest of, and the returns were kept under absolute control of, the parties in power. "Under such circumstances," asserted the memorial, "voting is a form and election a mockery."

Hon. William D. Porter, a prominent resident of Charleston, accompanied by a committee of representative citizens of the State, presented in an appropriate speech the Taxpayers' memorial to President Grant.

The President replied that he felt great sympathy for the people of South Carolina, who seemed to be badly governed and overtaxed, but that neither the executive nor the legislative branch of the National Government could do anything to better conditions. The remedy lay with the State of South Carolina which had a complete sovereign existence, and must make its own laws. The President added: "Where the fault lies, may be a question worth looking into. Whether a part of the excuse is not due to yourselves—whether it is not owing to the extreme views which you have held—whether your action has not consolidated the non-taxpaying portion of the community against you—are questions which I leave to your own consideration."

Not content to stop with these remarks, President Grant went on to say that a portion of his sympathy for South Carolina had been estranged by a speech made in the Taxpayers' Convention which he regarded as a slander upon himself. He

---

[116]Among the many frauds mentioned in the Taxpayers' memorial was the fact that in the single year of 1873 there had been actually paid to the clerks of the two houses for public printing the vast sum of $575,000, after which there was a large sum still due them, although they themselves admitted that the whole work was worth only $100,000; while others testified that it was worth only $50,000. The total appropriation for public printing for the sixty years of the State Government preceding the War of Secession was only $271,180—which was less by $60,765 than the amount paid for the same purpose by the Republicans in the single year of 1873.

referred to a speech of General M. W. Gary, of Edgefield, which criticized severely the President's official course toward South Carolina.   Not only had President Grant misconstrued a legitimate criticism of his official acts as a personal attack, but, in assigning it as the reason for his want of sympathy, he was using an incident that was extraneous to the matter which the committee was bringing to his attention as Chief Magistrate of the nation; namely, the deplorable condition of the people of one of the States.

When the committee retired it was with a feeling that they had met with a decided rebuff from the President and that their visit to him was a failure.

The Taxpayers' memorial was replied to by the Republican party in the State in a lengthy document, which, while admitting the enormous increase in the public debt, endeavored to account for it.   In this document the Republicans applied to the taxpayers the remark which had been made by Bismarck to certain of those who complained to him of the oppression of the Prussian laws: "Unfortunately, you are accustomed to complain of oppression when not permitted to lord it over others."   The members of the Taxpayers' Convention, according to the reply of the Republicans, were "the prominent politicians of the old regime—the former ruling element of the State, who simply desired to regain the power they lost by the folly of Secession."

The "reply" of the Republicans to the taxpayers was presented to the President by a committee of twenty-four members, at least fourteen of whom had been guilty of bribery, while all of the others had been actively associated with the spoilers in South Carolina.[117]

The President stated that the "reply" seemed to be conclusive.   The Republican majorities of the committees of the Senate and House, before whom the taxpayers' committee had also appeared, reported that the subject matter contained in the memorial was beyond the jurisdiction of Congress.

The Democratic minority of the House Committee, however, recommended that Congress should act in the matter, saying:

"The cry of that outraged, helpless and suffering people has reached our hearts as well as our understanding.   That once

[117]Reynolds, p. 262.

prosperous and beautiful State is on the verge of ruin. She is indeed already prostrate. A horde of thieves and robbers, worse than any that has ever infested any civilized community on earth, have her by the throat, and are fast sucking her life-blood. Three hundred thousand of her citizens, descendants of those who fought and won with our fathers the battles of American liberty, are crying to Congress for redress—for help. They have exhausted every resource, and are of themselves utterly helpless. To refuse their request is to drive them to despair and ruin."

Early in September, 1874, when the election was drawing near, Senator Patterson went to Washington and made a further appeal for troops. He told the President, according to the newspapers, that terrorism existed among the negroes and white Republicans in South Carolina; that murders and outrages were of almost daily occurrence, and that he feared a war of the races; that those who led in the Ku Klux outrages were reorganizing and drilling rifle clubs all over the State; and that no Republicans were admitted to these organizations. He added that the only hope for the State was in the Federal army being distributed throughout South Carolina and held there until after the election.

Republican politicians from other Southern States made to the President charges against their respective States similar to those made by Patterson against South Carolina. Accepting the charges as true, President Grant addressed a letter to the Attorney-General of the United States, saying that "the recent atrocities in Alabama, Louisiana and South Carolina showed a disregard for law, civil rights and personal protection that ought not to be tolerated in any civilized government." The department commanders in the South then received orders for such a disposition of their troops as would meet the situation as it had been presented to the Executive.

Meanwhile, in accordance with the recommendation of the Taxpayers Convention, the taxpayers in each county had formed a County Tax Union to look after their interests. When news of President Grant's action reached the State, General James Chestnut of Camden, State Chairman, called a State convention of delegates from the County Tax Unions. The convention assembled in Columbia on September 10, and appointed a committee to investigate the charges which the President had made against South Carolina. After a thorough investigation this committee made a report, which is so important that it is quoted somewhat at length:

We have failed to ascertain a single case in the State of an injury, outrage or wrong committed during the present year by a white man upon a negro in the slightest degree attributable to the race, color or previous condition of servitude of the negro, or upon any Republican on account of his political opinions. * * *

We deem it, however, not irrelevant to report that a conflict of races has only been avoided by the uniform forbearance of the whites. * * *

The tendency to a conflict exists entirely on the side of the negroes, and arises from the existence of the following condition of affairs: * * * The negro is taught to consider that the whites (except Republicans) have not the right to form volunteer military organizations, and hence regard the rifle clubs lately formed, for martial, social and defensive purposes, the evidence of incipient rebellion. The fact that almost the entire militia of the State are negroes, and that white companies have not been accepted by the State authorities where tendered, may have caused this opinion. The negro militia are commanded by turbulent officers, are armed with fine arms, and abundantly supplied with ball cartridges, as if their services in actual conflict might any day be required. * * *

The carpetbaggers (by which term we do not mean those from other States who remove here, but the dishonest political adventurers who now infest this State) do everything in their power by incendiary speeches, slanders and otherwise to inflame the blacks against any of their own color who might dare to vote as they call it "against their race." Thus, there is no political freedom in South Carolina for either race, and little civil liberty for the whites. It is true, and it could not be otherwise, that there exists a feeling of deep indignation on the part of the whites, but it is not against the negro, nor against the honest Republicans of either color, but against those who have organized a system of election frauds; invent and publish abroad shameful slanders for political purposes; crush us with taxes; steal the money raised by taxation; teach the negro the infamous doctrines above mentioned, and in general teach the negroes to regard all white men not of the Republican party as their natural enemies.

Late in September, 1874, trouble occurred in Edgefield County. The trouble grew out of the conduct of Ned Tennent, a negro captain of militia, who, declaring that his house had been fired into the night before by unknown parties, called out his military company, as he alleged, for protection. About three hundred negroes assembled under arms, whereupon General M. C. Butler organized a large force of whites to meet them. A parley ensued in which Tennent was very defiant. Holding out his hand, which was filled with cartridges, he announced his intention "to kill and to burn." He was finally placed under arrest, charged with rioting, and his followers then dispersed. Some days later Tennent went to Edgefield with his company and delivered up their arms to the United States troops stationed there. A second negro company following this example shortly afterwards, the trouble in Edgefield came to an end.

Two days after this disturbance Governor Moses wired to the President that a reign of terror existed in Edgefield County, and added: "I ask that you will send immediate orders to Colonel H. M. Black, commanding the United States forces in Columbia, to report to me with such of his command as it may be found necessary to employ, as speedily as possible."

For once, however, the War Department failed to respond to the demand for further troops, holding that the company already at Edgefield was sufficient to handle the situation.

Moses' conduct while Governor had become so notorious all over the country, and his deeds of villainy were so brazen, that the carpetbag leaders in South Carolina received notice that they would be abandoned by the National Republican Party and by the National Government, which furnished the bayonets that held the white people in place, unless the party in South Carolina would drop Moses and otherwise undergo reformation. The Radical leaders in the State, both white and negro, took the cue, and began to cry out for reform, though with no idea of abandoning the political machine through which they had obtained control of the State.

CHAPTER XII

The "Reform" Republican Governor

The Republican organization of South Carolina, still professing an intention to "clean house," held its convention of 1874 with reform as the watchword of its delegates and as the keynote of its platform. The convention nominated D. H. Chamberlain for Governor, and renominated the negro Gleaves for Lieutenant Governor. Chamberlain, in accepting the nomination in a polished speeech, pledged the party to retrenchment, reform and good government.

Many Republicans, both white and black, not believing Chamberlain a fit man to accomplish reform, refused to accept him as their standard bearer. Styling themselves Independent Republicans they held a convention and nominated John T. Green, of Sumter, Judge of the Third Circuit, as their candidate for Governor. For Lieutenant Governor they named Martin R. Delany, a negro of Charleston. In resolutions which they adopted they called on all voters who sincerely desired good government, irrespective of party affiliations, to join them in the redemption of the State from the "corrupt rings which have disgraced the Republican party and trampled upon the interests of the Republicans and Conservatives alike."

As the Democrats (Conservatives) could see no difference between Chamberlain and his associates who had debauched the State, they were no more convinced by his promises of refrom than were the Independent Republicans, and were therefore, no more pleased at his nomination. The Democratic State Convention, deeming it inexpedient to put out a ticket, endorsed the candidates of the Independent Republicans in resolutions which declared that the "regular nominating convention of the Republican party has nominated for Governor and Lieutenant Governor men whose antecedents show them to be unworthy of confidence and whose success would insure the continuance of the corruption, dishonesty and party tyranny which have prostrated the State"; while the independent wing of the Republican party has "made nominations of men whose antecedents entitle them to confidence in their integrity and honesty."

Of the nominees of the Independent Republicans, thus endorsed by the Democrats, it may be said: Judge Green, the candidate for Governor, though of that small band of natives that joined the Republican party, was a man of integrity and he stood high as a lawyer. Delany, candidate for Lieutenant Governor, was an interesting character of the carpetbag regime, whose career was so unusual as to deserve especial notice.

Delany was a full-blooded negro, a native of the part of Virginia that is now West Virginia. With but little preparatory education he was able to graduate from the Harvard Medical School, while from extensive traveling in Europe he acquired considerable culture. Becoming prominent in the anti-slavery movement in the United States he proved himself a man of unusual intelligence and a good speaker, though, on account of the extreme views on the race question to which he gave utterance while fighting slavery, he had aroused an antipathy for himself among the whites, especially in the South.[118]

Delany held the rank of major of infantry in the United States Army when he first came to South Carolina. Then he became connected with the Freedmen's Bureau, and in this capacity, he made a favorable impression on the white people of the State, who regarded him as honest—something out of the ordinary for a carpetbagger. At the time of his nomination for Lieutenant Governor he was a practicing physician in Charleston.

[118]Both the grandfathers of Delany were African chiefs, and Delany himself was distinguished as a central African explorer. After meeting him on one occasion, President Lincoln remarked to Secretary Stanton: "Do not fail to have an interview with this most extraordinary and intelligent colored man." Delany, on account of his scientific attainments, received a royal commission as delegate from England to the Internation Statistical Congress held in London in the summer of 1860. The Congress was presided over by his Royal Highness, Albert, Prince Consort of England, and was attended by intellectual and distinguished representatives from all the nations of the civilized world. Delany, who had won the friendship of the great Lord Brougham, was formally presented by him to the Congress at the first day's session. Judge A. B. Long street, the celebrated author of "Georgia Scenes," who was at the time President of the South Carolina College, was present as the delegate to represent the United States, having been appointed by President Buchanan. Longstreet, holding that the attention shown Delany at the Congress was intended as an insult to this country, withdrew from the body immediately.—From Frank A. Bollin's Life and Public Services of Major Martin R. Delany, p. 100.
One of the first official acts of Hampton, after he became Governor, was to appoint Delany a trial justice (magistrate) for the city of Charleston.

In his canvass of the State for the office of Lieutenant Governor, Delany inveighed strongly against the official corruption which was going on, and warned the negroes to look to the future, taking the position that those who had given "liberty and equality of rights to the blacks had no desire to see them rule over their own race." "Rest assured," he said, "that there are no white people, North or South, who will submit that the black rule over the white in America."[119]

The election of 1874 passed off without any untoward incident, the Federal troops remaining quietly in their quarters in the various towns of the State which they garrisoned. The Chamberlain-Gleaves ticket was victorious by a majority of 11,000—which was very small when compared to the 33,000 majority which had been polled by both Scott and Moses. That the majority for the Chamberlain ticket was no larger was due to the fact that the white people voted for Green and Delany. Professor Davis calls attention to the fact that, if this ticket had been successful, the white people of South Carolina would have had for their Governor a full-blooded negro elected by their votes, as Judge Green died shortly after the election.[120]

Chamberlain, in his inaugural address, which was a long and able document, called attention to the fact that the two political parties in the State presented the same platform, notwithstanding that they were widely separated in political sympathies and aims. The paramount duty, he said, was the enforcement of economy and honesty in administration of the government, and he suggested ways for bringing about this much to be desired condition.

In concluding his inaugural address, the Governor said: "The work which lies before us is serious beyond that which falls to the lot of most generations of men. It is nothing less than the re-establishment of society in this State upon the foundations of absolute equality of civil and political rights. The evils attending our first steps in this work have drawn upon us the frowns of the whole world. Those who opposed the policy upon which our State was restored to her practical relations with the Union have already visited us with the ver-

---

[119]Taylor (negro), p. 210; Charleston *News and Courier,* February 13, October 3, 1874.
[120]Davis' manuscript.

dict of absolute condemnation. Those who framed and enforced that policy are filled with anxiety for the result, in which fear often predominates over hope. The result, under Divine Providence, rests with us."

Governor Chamberlain followed up his inaugural address by messages to the Legislature urging many reforms. But the appeals fell upon deaf ears. The political party that had elected him Governor was too strong for him—its leaders were too steeped in corruption and too firmly entrenched in their leadership. In fact, it was through the distribution of some of the plunder among their lieutenants that they held their power. At the very time that the party elected Chamberlain Governor it chose the most evil and corrupt Legislature that the State has ever had—a Legislature in no humor to pay much attention to the Governor's recommendations for reforms. On the other hand, though Chamberlain vetoed some of the objectionable measures passed by the Legislature, he approved many extravagent appropriations after he had condemned them.

Meanwhile, public scandals continued to shock the decent people of the State. Soon after Chamberlain's administration began, his enemies in his own party sought to stab him through his friend, F. L. Cardoza, the State Treasurer. A resolution was introduced into the Legislature demanding that the Governor remove Cardoza for malfeasance in office and neglect of duty. After considerable debate the resolution was lost. The result was regarded as a decided triumph for Chamberlain, who declared his complete belief in Cardoza's honesty and integrity, and averred that the movement was a "conspiracy to knock down one of the strongest pillars of the present reform administration." Cardoza, a mulatto preacher, was a graduate of the University of Edinburgh, and a man of much ability. After the Democrats regained control he was convicted of having defrauded the State, but was pardoned by Governor Hampton.

In the summer of 1875 the failure of Hardy Solomon's "bank," known as the South Carolina Bank and Trust Company, was announced. This so-called "bank" was in reality only one of the many schemes devised during Scott's administration for plundering the State Treasury. In Moses' term as Governor the sum of $125,000 had been appropriated to pay the fraudulent claims of this institution. To secure the passage of the measure, however, Solomon had to pay out $80,000 in the form of bribes to the members of the Legislature. During a period of less than five months—from January 9th to June 2nd, 1875—the day on which the "bank" suspended payment and closed its doors, the State deposits had increased from $11,000 to $205,000, all of which was lost in the "failure."[121]

At the time this increase of the State's deposits was made, Solomon's bank was reputed to be in an unsound condition, and for this reason State Treasurer Cardozo, one of the three State officials constituting the board of deposit, voted against putting more of the State's money in the bank, but Governor Chamberlain and the third member of the board voted in favor of it. After the failure, when the Legislature asked the board of deposit for an explanation, Chamberlain replied that he was ignorant of the bank's insolvency when he voted to increase the State's deposit; but he failed to explain satisfactorily how he came to be unaware of a fact that was well known not only to another member of the board, the State Treasurer, but to others outside the board.

Niles G. Parker, the notorious former State Treasurer, who, it will be remembered, was one of the "bond ring," and, with Scott and Chamberlain, was more or less implicated in Kimpton's nefarious bond transactions, had been in close quarters many times on account of his persistent stealing, but had succeeded in escaping punishment. He began, however, in 1875 to get into serious trouble.

Judgment for $75,000 was obtained against Parker in the civil courts of Richland County. Other actions were then brought against him, and on one of them he was placed in jail. After a few weeks he managed to break jail and make his escape. Two weeks later he was captured, but after another short imprisonment he was released. Arrested on still another charge, he was admitted to bail in the sum of $2,000 on a worthless bond, and fled the State. Property of Parker's val-

---

[121]Hardy Solomon, a white man, who was utterly devoid of character, also conducted a grocery store in Columbia, and furnished a large portion of the "supplies"—wines, liquors, and cigars—with which the "statesmen" regaled themselves at the expense of the taxpayer.

ued at $15,000 was seized by the State and the cases against him ended there.[122]

Chamberlain's enemies in his own party charged him with the responsibility for the drastic measures which had been taken against Parker, his former colleague on the Financial Board, the medium through which the "bond ring" worked. They alleged that Chamberlain's zeal in the matter, as in other matters of the same kind, was prompted by his desire to win the Democratic endorsement in his candidacy for re-election in 1876. Afterwards Parker bitterly arraigned Chamberlain before the Democratic Legislative Investigating Committee in 1877. He told of a disreputable deal which he alleged had taken place between them, while Chamberlain was seeking the nomination for Governor in 1874, as the price of his (Parker's) silence in regard to Chamberlain's part in the juggling of the State's bonds by the Financial Board. No sooner, however, claimed Parker, had Chamberlain been inaugurated, than he turned upon his quondam colleague and friend. Chamberlain, who was living in New York at the time this charge was made, denied it absolutely.

The Republicans of South Carolina had now had years of experience in controlling the public affairs of the State, yet they knew that their government was still unable to stand without the support of United States soldiers. As an excuse for asking for the retention of Federal troops, they had from the first spread abroad false stories of killings and other outrages committed by the Southern whites upon the negroes solely because the negroes voted the Republican ticket; while, as a matter of fact, the restraint of the whites, remarkable in the face of the aggressiveness of the negroes, alone prevented serious trouble between the races.

Radical newspapers and Radical leaders in the North, realizing that these stories made good campaign material for the Republican party throughout the country, loudly denounced the "outrages" in the South. This method of firing the

---

[122]The three-story building in Columbia next to the City Hall, now designated as 1209 Main Street, was erected by Parker with money which he stole from the State. The words "Parker's Hall" were originally displayed on the front of this building near the top, but they were taken down when the newspapers began to call it "Parker's Haul." The name was then changed to "Parker's Block," which the newspapers promptly altered to "Parker's Stumbling Block." Under the judgment against Parker this building was levied on and became the property of the State. It was used for the Agricultural Department from 1877 until about the year 1892, when the State sold it.

Northern heart against the white people of the South became known as "waving the bloody shirt."[123]

Although there had been no disorder in the State at the time of Chamberlain's inauguration, yet the Legislature, early in its first session, passed the usual resolutions, asking that the United States soldiers be retained in the State, and giving as the reason that "the peaceful and law-abiding citizens of this State desire that no opportunity be given for domestic violence or bloodshed, and the presence of the Federal troops is a restraint to organized and disciplined conspirators and disturbers of the public peace."

Early in 1875, soon after the passage of this resolution, trouble occurred again in Edgefield County, and again the origin of the trouble was due to Ned Tennant, the negro captain who had once more come to the front. Tennant's company had received back from Lawrence Cain, Senator from Edgefield, who was also a colonel in the negro militia, the rifles which they had delivered up to the authorities in September, 1874. The company thereupon took up their nightly drills again, and their conduct showed that Tennant was instigating them to bring on trouble by inciting the whites. The riotous conduct of Tennant's company finally became so unbearable that a warrant was issued by the civil authorities for his arrest. Several clashes occurred between the militia and the sheriff's possee before Tennant was arrested and put in jail.

A few days later the Governor sent T. J. Mackey, Judge of the Sixth Circuit, to inquire into conditions in Edgefield.[124] Mackey reported that: "No such iniquity as the county govern-

---

[123]The expression, "waving the bloody shirt," is said to have had its origin in an incident occurring in a speech made in the United States Senate by Senator D. P. Morton, of Indiana, in support of one of the "Force Bills," in which he assailed the Southern white people very bitterly, charging them with the most diabolical outrages committed upon negroes for political reasons. In the course of his diatribe he held aloft, for the view of the Senators, a blood-stained shirt which he alleged was taken from the body of a negro killed in the South by whites, solely because of his politics.

[124]Mackey, a native white Republican, had by his offensive partisanship made himself particularly distasteful to the white people of the State. He was a man of misdirected ability who was strangely lacking in the higher attributes of character. With a deep, sonorous voice, and remarkable conversational powers, he drew a crowd around him wherever he went. He had a ready Irish wit, and a keen, though perverted, sense of humor, which he often used in the court-room with the effect of lowering the dignity of the bench and making a travesty of justice. Some of his witty sayings are quoted by the lawyers of the State to this day.

ment of Edgefield has been inflicted upon any portion of the
English-speaking race since the Saxon wore the iron collar
of the Norman. . . . The condition of Edgefield presents a
problem that demands an instant solution in the interests of
public peace and the due preservation of life and property."
Judge Mackey later amplified his report with the statement
that, "the government of Edgefield has been for eight years a
festering ulcer upon our body politic, and a diligent attempt
is now being made to hide with the 'bloody shirt' the appalling
wrongs committed by the Republican party on the white population of that section. For example, there have been three
county treasurers, all Republicans, appointed in Edgefield since
1868. The first, John Wooley, proved a defaulter to the
amount of $25,000; the second, Eichelberger, in the sum of
about $30,000; and the third, McDevitt, estimated at $40,000
or $50,000."

Acting upon recommendations contained in Judge Mackey's
report, Governor Chamberlain issued a proclamation disbanding
all the negro militia companies in Edgefield County, and re-
quiring them to turn in their arms, ammunition, and equipment; and, at the same time, commanding "all military organizations now existing in said county, not forming a part of
the State militia, nor sanctioned by the commander-in-chief
(rifle clubs), forthwith to disband and henceforth to cease
from assembling, arming, drilling, parading, or otherwise en-
gaging in any military exercises." The Governor's proclamation was obeyed, and quiet was restored to Edgefield.[125]

The pleas for reform that Chamberlain made in his inaugural
address and in his subsequent messages to the Legislature had
the ring of sincerity—so much so, that, despite his former
intimate association with the robbers, white and black, and,
despite the fact that some of his acts as Governor were open
to severe criticism, many of the white people had, by the end
of the first year of his administration, come to have confidence in Chamberlain and to believe that, with the right kind
of Legislature, he would accomplish much good. Most of the
Democratic press of the State gave him high praise, and
assured him of their support in his efforts for reform. By
invitation of the white people, Chamberlain addressed many

---

[125]Reynolds, pp. 301-302.

colleges and civic, patriotic and social societies in the State; and, interest in his call for good government having spread afar, he also addressed many audiences beyond the borders of the State. These addresses were all scholarly, and added greatly to Chamberlain's reputation at home and abroad.

CHAPTER XIII

THE CROWNING INFAMY OF THE RADICAL LEGISLATURE

The Legislature, in December, 1875, while in its second session in Chamberlain's administration, elected W. J. Whipper, a Northern negro, and F. J. Moses, Jr., as Judges of the First and Third Circuits, respectively. Comment upon the character of Moses is unnecessary, and Whipper was no better than Moses; in fact, they were well matched. Whipper, who was a leader of his race, was utterly without character. None of the State's plunderers was more insolent, bold or defiant, and many of the disturbances between the whites and blacks are traceable to Whipper's baleful influence upon the members of his race.[126] Owing to the fact that the Circuit Judges did not rotate then as now, a man like Whipper or Moses could have made himself a petty despot in his jurisdiction.[127]

Governor Chamberlain promptly denounced the election of Whipper and Moses as "a horrible disaster—a disaster equally great to the State and to the Republican party—a calamity infinitely greater than any which has yet fallen on this State or any part of the South * * * [for] neither Whipper nor Moses has any qualities which approach to a qualification for judicial positions. The reputation of Moses is covered deep with charges, which are believed by all who are familiar with the facts, of corruption, bribery and utter prostitution of all his official powers to the worst possible purposes."

The Governor, having been invited to attend a supper given by the New England Society in Charleston on Forefathers' Day, December 22, shortly after the election of Whipper and Moses, wired the Society: "I cannot attend your annual supper

---

[126]In marked contrast to Whipper's generally bad character was his attitude in advocacy of woman suffrage in the Constitutional Convention in 1868. In an able speech he asserted that he was convinced of the superiority of women; that many of them had exhibited greater intelligence than his own sex, and that he considered it "unjust, contemptible, and wrong to deprive these intelligent beings of the privileges which were common to men." Until women were recognized as the political equals of men, Whipper asserted, governments laid on insecure foundations would never become permanent. From this issue, he continued, there was no escape, and he predicted that the agitation of it would continue until it would ultimately prevail.—Taylor, p. 142.

It will be remembered that at the time of the adoption of the Nineteenth Amendment to the Constitution providing for woman suffrage, there were many in the South who feared its possible effects in the future, since, of course, it enfranchised the women of both races.

[127]Davis' manuscript.

tonight; but if there ever was an hour when the spirit of the Puritan, the spirit of undying and unconquerable enmity and defiance to wrong, ought to animate their sons, it is this hour, here, in South Carolina. The civilization of the Puritan and the Cavalier, of the Roundhead and the Huguenot, is in peril. Courage, determination, union, victory must be the watchword. The grim Puritans never quailed under threat or blow. Let their sons now imitate their example. God bless the New England Society."

The Governor's telegram when read to the Society evoked much enthusiasm, the band playing "Hail to the Chief." General James Simons, a typical Charlestonian of the old school, responding in the Governor's absence, to the toast to South Carolina, said of the State's Chief Magistrate: "You have a man ruling over your State who has the affection, the respect, the esteem and the confidence of the people"—a sentiment which met with hearty response from his audience.

While the press of the entire country, of both political parties, condemned the action of the Legislature in most unmeasured terms, a storm of indignation swept over South Carolina, and the State boiled and seethed like a cauldron. "Seldom has any community in modern times received such a shock." [128]

Acting on a construction of the law which the State Supreme Court afterwards sustained, Chamberlain refused to commission Whipper and Moses. Meetings were held in all parts of the State to protest against the elections and to endorse Chamberlain's stand.

At an indignation meeting held in Charleston, in the First Circuit, where Whipper was to preside, Hon. B. C. Pressley, afterwards a Democratic Judge of the circuit, declared: "I tell you that we have drunk the last drop of the bitter cup that we intend to drink, unless the United States Army says so. . `. . So, fellow citizens, Governor Chamberlain may go to sleep and sleep soundly—for they don't dare to touch a hair of his head, for the people are awake and they are not going to sleep again! The time has come for action! There must be no mental reservation when we say that we will stand by Governor Chamberlain. * * * Stand up for your civilization, your property, your lives, and your honor!"

[128]Walter Allen's Governor Chamberlain's Administration in South Carolina, p. 198.

At a meeting at Sumter, in the Third Circuit, where Moses was to preside, Hon. T. B. Fraser, afterwards a Democratic Judge of the Circuit, declared: "It is one of the purposes of this meeting to announce that F. J. Moses, Jr., shall never take a seat in our courthouse, unless placed there by Federal bayonets." He was followed by Charles H. Moise, Esq., a leading member of the Sumter bar, who made the pledge: "Should F. J. Moses, Jr., by any legal trickery, attempt to ascend the steps of the courthouse to take his seat as judge, I, Charles H. Moise, forty-six years of age, with a wife and ten children to support, am ready to unite with a band of determined men, and with muskets on our shoulders defend that temple of justice from such a desecration."

A meeting of white citizens of Barnwell resolved: "That we heartily endorse Governor Chamberlain in his efforts to redeem the State from plunder and degradation, and while he has been faithful to his own party, he has also been faithful to ours, and we hereby pledge ourselves to stand by and support him promptly, faithfully, fearlessly and defiantly."

The election of two such men as Judges showed that the Legislature had sunk to the lowest depth, and, at the same time, it is one of the most momentous events connected with carpet-bag rule in South Carolina. Its importance in the history of the State cannot be overestimated. Public feeling ran so high that had Whipper and Moses attempted to preside in the Courts, the State would have been plunged into bloodshed before they would have been permitted to do so, and the whole subsequent history of South Carolina would have been changed.

The event was of significance in still another way. Chamberlain gained so much popularity among the white people of standing in the State by his course in this matter, that if the two political parties had held their conventions for the nomination of State offices at that time, instead of the following summer, it is safe to say that the Democrats (Conservatives) would not have made a nomination for Governor, but would have endorsed Chamberlain on a fusion ticket. Such a result would have been little short of a calamity, as it would probably have prolonged carpetbag rule indefinitely.

Professor Davis expresses the opinion that "this episode of the Judges should be carefully rated by the philosophic student of history. It fully explains the great popularity enjoyed by

Chamberlain in the spring of 1876, and is the keynote to the problem why so many good Conservatives desired a fusion with Chamberlain up to the time of the nomination of Hampton. * * * It was generally conceded at the time that Chamberlain was the arbiter of the State's destiny. * * * Chamberlain was the hero of the hour, and in Charleston and Sumter especially he was regarded as a champion and a deliverer. * * * South Carolina was enjoying its first calm in several years. People began to breathe more freely and to hope for the future." [129]

In attempting to form a judgment of the character of Chamberlain it should be said, in justice to him, that too much emphasis cannot be placed upon the fact that it would have been impossible for any one to accomplish much in the way of reform with the vast majority of office-holders corrupt and ignorant, and, consequently, hostile to everything that threatened to put an end to the "era of good stealing." The frauds already mentioned give an idea of the magnitude of the corruption. A few illustrations of illiteracy will suffice to show the extent of the ignorance of the negro office-holders, recently freed from slavery.

The public school system which so closely affects the welfare of the children—the future hope of a State—did not escape the blight of ignorance. One of the duties of the County School Commissioner (now called County Superintendent of Education) was, as Chairman of the Board of Examiners, to examine applicants for positions as teachers and recommend for appointment such as in his judgment were most suited. The negro School Commissioner of Richland County, in which is located the capital of the State, wrote the following recommendation of teachers, the correct orthography of the official heading being due to the fact that the heading was printed on his stationery:

County School Commissioner's Office
Richland County
Columbia, S. C., Sept. the 27 1871
The foller ring name person are Rickermended to the Boarde.
[Here follows a list of names.]
for the Hower [Howard (?) Schoole] Haveing Given fool sat es fact Shon in thi tow Last years
the whit Shool
[Another list of names.]

[129]Davis' manuscript.

A school trustee was required by law to employ teachers and approve their pay certificates. A negro school trustee of Barnwell County wrote to a merchant in Columbia:

Mr. ———— Pleas give to the Barrow for mee Dick Kenenedy one plug of To Baco and a Bar of soape i am Bussey my self trying to get a Bale of Cooton to you or i would acome.

The negro legislators averaged a no higher degree of literacy. A negro candidate for the House of Representatives from Marion County wrote the County Chairman of his (Republican) party:

Marion County S. C. August The 27 Mr. Chair man dear Sir Therse Lins will Inform you That I am well At This Time and Hoping That You The same Mr. C. Smith dear Sir I have Ben offort for a Representatives Please write Me Some Information I have ben Put to the House and Reserve 706 when Ben deas reserve 7 Please write to me whot you Think of my run writ soon.

The journals of the Legislature as they appear in the official records are expressed in good style. This seeming anomaly is explained by the fact that all proposed bills and resolutions were, before acted upon, put in proper form by educated persons.

A negro member from Colleton County introduced into the House the following resolution:

Resolved by the House of Representatives the Senate concurren, that whereas the leageslatures of South Carolina had conveane by his Excellency the Governor F. J. Moses, Jr., the 21 of Oct. 1873 for the purpose of the Reduction of the Bounding dept of the State.

and whereas the Leageslators are failed to imbracing the Bounding which is Required as a Servant to the People interest but from day after day introduce Bill and Resolution which is know servance to the people; therefor Be it Resolved that the House now adjourn sine die.

The resolution, after having been "edited," appears in the journal of the House as follows:

Whereas the Legislature of South Carolina was convened by his Excellency the Governor, Franklin J. Moses, Jr., on the 21st of October, 1873, for the purpose of reducing the bonded debt of the State; and whereas the Legislature has failed to take any measures tending to effect such reduction, which was a duty demanded of them as faithful servants of the people; and whereas bills and resolutions of no public interest are introduced day after day; therefore be it

Resolved by the House of Representatives, the State concurring, that the General Assembly adjourn this day *sine die*.[130]

To this day opinions differ in South Carolina in regard to Chamberlain. The fact that he was a man of extraordinary

---

[130]The writer is indebted for the specimens of illiteracy given in the text to Reynolds, pp. 122, 123, 335, 336. Shortly after his inauguration Chamberlain made the statement that upon assuming the Governorship he found two hundred trial justices (magistrates) who could neither read nor write.

ability and scholarly attainments made his career in South Carolina all the more incomprehensible Soon after coming to the State, he assumed leadership among the negroes, and made speeches to them which were well calculated to inflame them against the whites. He preached and practiced social equality between the races, insisting that they attend the same schools, and he voted to admit negroes to the State University.

During all the years of Reconstruction in South Carolina, except the two years of Moses' administration, Chamberlain was a member, or the legal advisor, of practically all the State boards, which the rings used as the mediums for plundering the State. If he was not involved in corruption himself, he was certainly very close to those who were.

It is inconceivable that Chamberlain, having supervision of every transaction of the various State boards, could have been ignorant of stealing of such gigantic proportions as was continually going on around him. As a matter of fact, the frauds were commonly known to the public at the time, and later the Democratic Legislative Investigating Committee had no difficulty in ferreting out many of the facts concerning them.

Those who hold to the more unfavorable view of Chamberlain's character, assert:

Chamberlain's inconsistency shows that his clamor for reform was insincere. While calling aloud for good government, he supported for office, and received favors from, notorious corruptionists. His appointments, while Governor, were not always good; and he approved extravagant appropriations that he had previously condemned.

Chamberlain's letter to Kimpton (Chapter VI), and the circumstances in the case of the bribery of J. J. Wright, the negro Associate Justice of the State Supreme Court,[131] prove his moral turpitude. No convincing evidence was brought out by the several investigating committees to connect Chamberlain with the plundering of the State because he was too smart to leave well-marked traces of his wrongdoing.[132]

---

[131]"That Chamberlain paid $2,500 to Moses [to be delivered to Wright] for the purpose of securing a favorable decision your committee have no doubt."— From report of the Democratic Legislative Investigating Committee, 1877–78.

[132]Numerous charges against Chamberlain were made to the Democratic Legislative Investigating Committee, 1877–78, but, as these charges came from self-confessed thieves, little or no credence is given them. Chamberlain wrote in reply to the charges: "To every specific and general charge involving moral delinquency or conscious wrong in my official action in this State I give my absolute and solemn denial."

If a man be judged by the company he keeps, Chamberlain stands convicted so far as his career in South Carolina is concerned, for here "his closest associates were from among the very lowest products of the Reconstruction period." His later career in the North was but another phase of his insincerity. His purpose there was to regain for himself the good opinion of mankind that his intellectuality craved.

An editorial judgment of the *Columbia* (S. C.) *Register,* though written when the feeling engendered by Reconstruction was bitter, still voices the sentiment of many South Carolinians:

"Like other carpetbaggers concerned in the wholesale robbery of the State, Daniel H. Chamberlain lacked both money and principles when he went a needy adventurer from the North. Unlike his pals, he was a shrewd, clear-headed and far-seeing man, with the manners of a gentleman and the intellectual habits of a scholar. Being incomparably the ablest of the lot, he was by far the most dangerous * * * [for most of the time] every measure intended to filch money from the pockets of the taxpayers passed directly under his eye, and it were strange, indeed, that so keen a mind should fail to grasp the iniquity of his associates, when the rudest comprehension took in the true situation. * * * Whenever legislation was necessary to promote the schemes of plunder, it was Chamberlain's brain which concocted the law to blind the people to its true intent and meaning. * * * [But] he was too shrewd and calculating to become entangled with the rabble." [133]

But there is another view of Chamberlain's character. It is claimed for him that when he came to South Carolina he was a young idealist, fresh from the walls of Yale and Harvard and imbued with the spirit of abolitionism that pervaded his New England home. He brought with him the belief that political and civil rights would, within themselves, and within a short time, make the negro proficient in statecraft and elevate his position in the social structure. His ideals were soon shattered, however, as he wrote in 1871 to William L. Trenholm, a prominent citizen of Charleston, "three years have passed and the result is—what? Incompetence, dishonesty, corruption in all its forms have 'advanced their miscreant fronts';

[133]From issues of September 28, 1877, and December 8, 1878.

have put to flight the small remnant that opposed them, and now rule the party which rules the State."

The judgment of those who think better of Chamberlain, as to why he continued to affiliate with a government that had become rotten to the core, is summed up in the conclusion of Prof. Davis, written after the passion aroused by Reconstruction had had time to cool: "As Attorney General under Scott, he [Chamberlain] was ex officio member of several boards. These boards were known at the time, and subsequently proven, to have swindled and robbed without limit. While other members of the boards were reveling in ill-gotten gains, Chamberlain was apparently in moderate circumstances, and moved along quietly and unostentatiously. No stolen money was ever traced to him, and he positively denied any participation in the proceeds of public rascality. * * * The simplest explanation of this enigma is that Chamberlain did not attend the meetings of the Boards, and refused to participate in their work, while not revealing their frauds. This is not a very high position to take, but Chamberlain was young, he had a future before him, and in 1868-70 it seemed as if nothing could stay the flood. After a careful study of the question for years, this is my conclusion."[134]

For his part, the author of this book can only repeat the statement which he made in the opening chapter: Chamberlain will go down in the history of the State as the human paradox of the Reconstruction era—a man whose character was made up of contradictions and whose motives have never been satisfactorily explained.

---

[134]Davis' manuscript.

CHAPTER XIV

FUSION WITH CHAMBERLAIN LOSES OUT

The election year, 1876, opened with Chamberlain in such favor with many of the white people on account of his efforts while Governor for reform that it seemed highly improbable that the Democrats would put forward a candidate to run against him if he were nominated by the Republicans. It was urged that, with the overwhelming majority of negro voters in the State, the election of a Democratic Governor was impossible, and that therefore it would be better for the Democrats to acquiesce in Chamberlain's serving another term, and to center on a fight to secure a decent Legislature, for which the chances of success were good and without which a Governor could accomplish but little. A further consideration was the fact that 1876 was also a year for the election of a President of the United States. The National Republican party had, on account of scandals in the National administration and quarrels within the party, lost ground heavily throughout the country, and, as a consequence, the prospect of electing a Democratic President was particularly bright. With a Democrat in the Presidential chair, the State would be relieved of much of her woe. Yet, there was danger that the intense feeling that would be aroused throughout the State by a contest for a State ticket might bring on clashes between the races which would help in other sections of the country the chances of the Republican, and hurt the chances of the Democratic, candidate for President. They who argued in this way became known as the "conservative" wing of the Democratic party. They were undoubtedly patriots—men whose courage would dare anything that was necessary, but whose prudence cautioned them to avoid what to them seemed rashness. Underneath the restraint of expediency and in spite of it, every "conservative" in his heart, longed for a straight fight against the robbers who had fastened themselves upon the State.

Colonel Thomas Y. Simons, of Charleston, the South Carolina member of the National Democratic Executive Committee, having issued the call, the members of the State Central Committee met in Columbia early in January to arrange for the reorganization of the party for the approaching campaign. The Central Committee in an address to the people of South Carolina paid a tribute to Chamberlain's record as Governor, which, when compared with the party platform's denunciation of him two years previously, shows how Chamberlain's reputation had risen in that short time:

In common with their fellow citizens, the State Democratic Committee have watched with anxious solicitude and growing confidence the course of the present Governor of the State. They recognize and appreciate the value of what he has done, promoting reform and retrenchment during the past year. They applaud his wise and patriotic conduct in exerting his whole official power and personal influence for the undoing of the infamous judicial election, and they declare their belief that the Democracy of the State, rising above party, as he has done, will give an unfaltering support to his efforts as Governor for the redress of wrongs, for the reduction of taxation, to obtain a just administration of the law, and make the State Government a faithful guardian of the public and private interests of the people.

Most of the Democratic newspapers of the State advocated accepting Chamberlain. The leader among them was the Charleston *News and Courier,* edited by Francis W. Dawson, one of the most facile and forcible newspaper writers of the day, who had an honorable record for service in the Confederate army. In giving the arguments in favor of a coalition with Chamberlain, the *News and Courier* cited that Chamberlain as Governor had improved the character of the appointive officers and had exercised judiciously the pardoning power; had stabilized the public debt and had safeguarded the State's funds deposited in banks; had reduced the expenses of the State government and had lowered taxes. Then, after giving many reasons why, in its judgment, Chamberlain could not possibly be defeated, including the fact that the election machinery was in the hands of Republicans accustomed to manipulating elections to suit themselves, the *News and Courier* added: "How could he and his party be defeated? Only by *Armed Force.* For that the people are not ready, and if they were their attempts would result in disaster. * * * What we advise then is not to make Chamberlain under any circumstances a Democratic candidate, but to waive a nomination for Governor *if the regular Republicans* nominate him. * * * Whether the colored voting majority in the State be twenty thousand or thirty thousand, it is certainly large, and exceedingly difficult to overcome. The difficulty is increased by the fact that the colored population is massed in the lower counties where the whites are few, and the Radical majority can be made whatever the commissioners and managers of election choose to make it."

While the coalition movement was strongest in the low country, where the negro majority was overwhelming, the sentiment of the Winnsboro *News and Herald* expressed the opinion of probably the greater number of people of the up-country, at the beginning of 1876: "Governor Chamberlain is a necessity—meaning by that that in the condition of National and State politics a Democrat could not win, while a Republican who had the confidence of Northern Republicans could by the aid of South Carolina Conservatives accomplish much good."

According to Professor Davis: "Whatever then be the motive—whether a sincere admiration for Chamberlain—an acceptance of him to avoid something worse, or as a wedge to break forever the Republican party—the fact remains that, in the spring of 1876, fusion, to the extent of at least not opposing the re-election of Chamberlain as Governor, but of endeavoring to secure a Democratic Legislature, was the idea of a large majority of the white voters." [135]

On the other hand, the "Straightouts"—the Democrats who favored nominating a full State ticket—were, though they were as yet few in numbers, making themselves heard. Not having faith in the sincerity of Chamberlain's professions of reform, and fearing that, if given another lease of power, he would prove himself as bad as the other Republican Governors, they clamored for a straightout fight for every office "from Governor to Coroner," that the whole gang of thieves might be cleared out, "bag and baggage."

Meantime, opposition to Chamberlain had developed within his own party. His efforts at reform threatened to cut off the avenues to "good stealing"; so the most debased faction, the unmitigated rogues, objected to giving him further opportunity to continue a course so much to their disliking. They denounced him for having turned traitor to his party by going over to the enemy. Among the Republicans leading the opposition to Chamberlain's administration were the notorious ring-

---

[135]Davis' manuscript.

ster, John J. ("Honest John") Patterson, who had bought a seat in the United States Senate; R. B. Elliott, a negro, who had been a member of Congress and later Speaker of the South Carolina House of Representatives, and who, in office and out, was grossly corrupt and immoral; and Judge R. B. Carpenter. This was the same Carpenter who had run for Governor against Scott, in 1870, as a "Reform" Republican on a fusion ticket with General M. C. Butler, and had been supported by the Democrats because they believed him to be better than most of his party. Carpenter had since repented of his "reform," and had been taken back into the Republican fold, and into the counsels of the very basest element of the party.

A Republican State Convention, held in Columbia in April, for the purpose of electing delegates to the Republican National Convention, furnished an occasion for a trial of strength between the Chamberlain and anti-Chamberlain factions. The initial test—the election of a temporary chairman of the convention—seemed to indicate that Chamberlain had lost control of his party, for he was defeated for the position by a negro from Williamsburg, S. A. Swails, by a vote of 80 to 40. As the convention progressed the supporters and opponents of the Governor had such a turbulent time of it that there was danger more than once of serious bloodshed. One of the delegates threw an inkstand at another's head and in the melee which ensued a chair was raised threateningly over the Governor, who would have been struck down but for the interference of his friends. Judge Carpenter made a speech full of invectives against the Governor. Chamberlain re-countered with a masterly reply that turned the final victory to him. He was elected a delegate at large to the National Convention over Patterson by 89 to 32—a vote that more than reversed the previous majority against him.

The victory of Chamberlain in the Republican convention made it practically certain that he would be given a renomination by his party, and the fact that to gain the victory he had to wage a bitter contest against the baser faction of the Republicans gave encouragement to the Conservative Democrats in their belief that, if elected, he would continue his efforts for reform despite opposition from within his own party. With renewed earnestness, therefore, they pressed their argument that the Democrats, before deciding on the

course to pursue in State politics, should wait to see whether
the Republicans would renominate Chamberlain—a policy that
soon became known as "watch and wait." [136]

In the month (May) following the meeting of the Republican State Convention, and pursuant to a call of the Democratic
State Central Committee, the Democrats held a State convention in Columbia, "for the purpose of appointing delegates to
the National Democratic Convention * * * to take such further
action as the convention shall deem proper and necessary."
Already by direction of the State Central Committee, Democratic clubs with large membership had been organized in
every county. These clubs, meeting at their respective county
seats, had elected the delegates to the State Convention, many
of whom were from among the ablest men of their sections
of the State.

On the floor of the convention General M. C. Butler and
General M. W. Gary scathingly denounced Chamberlain and
made eloquent appeals for the nomination of a straightout
State ticket. General Gary offered the following resolution:

Resolved, That the Democratic party, when they make nominations
for State offices, put a straightout ticket in the field.

The "watch and wait" policy, however, was still in the
ascendancy, and the best that the Straightouts could make of
the situation was to secure for the State Executive Committee,
which the convention had just named, authorization to call,
whenever it deemed proper, a convention of the Democratic
party to nominate candidates for State offices.

Soon trouble occurred in Aiken County, although in it citizens from both Edgefield and Aiken were involved, that gave
great impetus to the Straightout movement. Edgefield, which
had often been a storm center of the unrest that accompanied
carpetbag rule in South Carolina, came again to the forefront.
B. R. Tillman, afterwards a Democratic Governor of South
Carolina and a United States Senator, who lived in the troubled
section at the time and was very active in the Straightout
cause says that in 1876 there was a complete regiment of
negro militia in Edgefield County, which constituted a standing menace to that section of the State. "The feeling between
the races was so bitter," he added, "that it was evident that

---

[136]Compare the message of President Wilson to Congress December 27, 1913:
"We shall not, I believe, be obliged to alter our policy of watchful waiting."

there would be bloody clashes. . . . The conditions in the country along the Savannah River, near Augusta, had come to such a desperate pass on account of the negroes, that no man's life was safe and highway robbery was an everyday affair." [137]

The town of Hamburg, situated just across the Savannah River from Augusta, is in that section of Aiken County which had formed part of the county of Edgefield until just a few years before (1871), when the county of Aiken was created. Once a town of great importance on account of its river location, the building of the railroad across the river to Augusta had sounded its death knell. At the time of this narrative its population was composed almost exclusively of negroes and the management of the town's affairs was conducted by them altogether. The most direct route from the South Carolina side to Augusta ran through Hamburg and consequently it was frequently used. On July 4, 1876, less than a week after the Fort Moultrie Centennial in Charleston, where Hampton commanded the military and Chamberlain was an honorary guest, two young men of Edgefield, passing through Hamburg on their return from Augusta, became involved in a difficulty with Doc Adams, an inveterate hater of the whites, and his militia company, then on parade. The difficulty grew out of the insolence and overbearing conduct of the negroes. Warrants were sworn out for Doc Adams and some of his men on the charge of disorderly conduct and their cases, after some delay, were set finally for hearing on July 8, before the negro trial justice (magistrate) in Hamburg.

On the day for the hearings large crowds, white and black, gathered in Hamburg. Both sides were armed—the whites because they claimed that the negroes had threatened to lynch the white men who had sworn to the warrants, and the negroes because they claimed they feared the whites would attack them. Among the whites were Georgians who had come from Augusta to give help if needful to the South Carolinians. General Butler, who was present to appear at the hearings in the capacity of attorney, endeavored, for the purpose of preventing trouble, to persuade the negro militia company to turn in their guns to the State authorities, since it was generally recognized that the company was not a legally organized part of the militia.

[137]B. R. Tillman, The Struggle of '76 (pamphlet).

Following the refusal of the negroes to comply with General
Butler's suggestion, firing began. Which side started the firing
no one can say. The negroes sought protection in an abandoned warehouse, which they had been using as an armory, and
fired at the whites from its windows. The whites responded
with a fusilade against the building. One of the bullets of
the negroes hit its mark. McKie Merriwether, a popular young
man of Edgefield, fell dead, shot through the head. Up to this
time no negro had been killed, for the fusilade against the
warehouse had been without much effect. When, however, a
small cannon, brought over from Augusta, opened fire upon
the warehouse, the negroes fled from the building in terror.
As they ran the whites followed, killing one and capturing the
rest. The next morning the infuriated whites shot to death,
one at a time, as an example to other negroes, the five who
were believed to have been the ringleaders in the dreadful
affray. "Many things," General Butler afterwards said, "were
done on this terrible night which cannot be justified, but the
negroes 'sowed the wind and reaped the whirlwind.'"

News of the riot at Hamburg shocked the entire nation.
The press everywhere denounced the brutality of the white
people of South Carolina. Governor Chamberlain joined the
hue and cry. He, too, put the entire blame upon the whites,
characterizing the affair as "the Hamburg massacre," an act of
"atrocity and barbarism" that showed a "murderous and in-
human spirit." Making it appear that the riot was due to
political reasons, when politics had nothing to do with it,[138]
Chamberlain appealed to President Grant to send more United
States soldiers to South Carolina, and that complaisant executive promised them to him.

When further particulars of the riot came out, they showed
that the whites were not entirely to blame, if to blame at all.
Even the mass of negro testimony that was gathered showed
that much of the blame belonged to the negroes. Looking back
on the event, over a distance of fifty years, it would seem that
both sides were to blame—the negroes for beginning the difficulty and keeping it up, and the whites for carrying it as far
as they did. The fact remains that all the white citizens accused by a jury of twelve negroes of complicity in the killing

---

[138]E. L. Wells, Hampton and Reconstruction, 126.

stood ready for trial at any time, yet not one was brought to trial, although the courts were in the hands of Republicans.

The reaction from the Hamburg riot upon the people of South Carolina was electrical. Deep resentment filled them against the country at large, and against Governor Chamberlain in particular for their unjust accusations. Thousands upon thousands who had been inclined towards the "watch and wait" policy of the conservative Democrats were converted to the belief that the straightout Democrats were right—that fusion with Chamberlain would prove a delusion. Chamberlain's whole course in the Hamburg affair, especially his appeal to Grant for more troops, convinced them that he had in his heart such deep distaste and distrust for the white people of the State that he could not be depended upon to go far in co-operation with them, and in opposition to his own party, in bringing about good government; that therefore a fight should be made all along the line to drive out the despoilers of the State and traducers of her name. Thenceforth the straightout movement surged forward with the rush of a torrent. The State Democratic Executive Committee, caught in the current, called a State convention, for August 15, in Columbia, to nominate Democratic candidates for State offices.[139]

County after county elected delegations instructed to vote for the nomination of a full State ticket. The "watch and wait" policy still had, however, many adherents and they were able to win a considerable number of delegations, among them the large delegation from Charleston, where the negro majority was very heavy and where Chamberlain had made himself exceedingly popular by his having prevented Whipper from serving as Judge of the Circuit Court in which that county was situated. When the last county had acted, it was clear that a safe, though not large, majority of the votes of the convention had been won by the Straightouts.

---

[139]"The Hamburg riot, a tragic episode in the struggle for white supremacy, caused more wide-spread comment throughout the North and was more far-reaching in its influence upon the fortunes of the white people of South Carolina than anything of the kind which has ever occurred in the State. Congress appointed an Investigating Committee to take testimony, and the 'bloody shirt' was waved by the Northern press from one end of the country to the other. I express it as my deliberate judgment after careful consideration of all the facts as I know them that Butler's work in Hamburg was more far-reaching in its consequences and valuable in its results than any action of either of the other two men [Hampton or Gary]. * * * Butler, when fighting for his seat in the Senate, denied participation in the Hamburg riot except in its preliminary stage as a lawyer. He said that he had nothing to do with the killing of any of the negroes. This was literally true, but he had fired the fuse and exploded the bomb, and one of its consequences was the redemption of the State from negro rule."—From Tillman's The Struggle of '76 (pamphlet).

CHAPTER XV

WADE HAMPTON NOMINATED FOR GOVERNOR

From the time in 1875 that the Straightout movement started, Wade Hampton had been prominently mentioned as the Democratic candidate for Governor, should it be decided to nominate a straight State ticket. As the year of 1876 advanced, and the Straightouts gained great headway, more and more Hampton came to be looked upon as the one man in South Carolina to lead the whites to victory.

Hampton had spent, as was his custom, the winter months at the end of 1875 on his plantation in Mississippi, but had returned at the beginning of 1876 to his home near Columbia.[140] Early in the summer he had, on account of the condition of his health, gone to his summer home in Cashier's Valley, in North Carolina. While there he had been elected a delegate from Richland County to the August State Convention, and upon the earnest solicitation of his friends, he returned to Columbia in time to take his seat in the convention.

The Democratic State Convention met informally on the appointed day, August 15. On the next day the convention was organized with the election of General W. W. Harllee, of Marion, as President. Since General Harllee was known to favor the nomination of a full State ticket, his selection was regarded as a victory for the Straightouts and was greeted with much applause. The question of nominating a State ticket was, in view of the grave situation in the State, one that it was wiser that the Convention should not deliberate upon in public, and, therefore, the convention went into secret session. Behind closed doors, and for five and a half hours the question of a State ticket or no State ticket was debated. When the doors were opened to the public it was announced that it had been decided by a vote of 82 to 65 to make nominations for Governor and other State officers immediately. Thereupon, General Butler nominated Wade Hampton for Governor and the nomination was seconded by Robert Aldrich of Barnwell.

---

[140]Hampton's home in the sandhills, where he lived while Governor, was about two miles east of Columbia, on the Camden road. It was accidentally destroyed by fire in 1899. The property was afterwards acquired by B. L. Abney, of Columbia, who built a residence there.

DEMOCRATIC STATE TICKET—1876
FOUR OF THE ABOVE WERE GOVERNORS OF SOUTH CAROLINA—HAMPTON, SIMPSON,
HAGOOD AND THOMPSON

General Hampton ascended the speaker's stand and made an eloquent address, in which he modestly asserted that there were others who would make more available candidates than he. "I felt that my day was past," he added, in reference to his having served the State in the war, "and that in returning to my native State, I was like him who said: 'An old man whose heart is broken has come to lay his weary bones among you. Give me a little earth for charity.' I have claimed nothing from South Carolina but a grave in yonder churchyard. But I have always said that if I could serve her by word or deed, her men had only to call on me, and I would devote all my time, my energy and my life to her service."

At the conclusion of his address, and amid cheers, General Hampton retired from the hall. He was then nominated for Governor by acclamation, and the hall still ringing with outbursts of long-pent-up enthusiasm, the convention took a recess until the following day.

On re-assembling[141] the convention named by acclamation the rest of the State ticket as follows:

Lieutenant Governor—W. D. Simpson, Laurens.

Secretary of State—R. M. Sims, of York.

Attorney-General—James Conner, of Charleston;[142]

State Superintendent of Education—Hugh S. Thompson, of Richland;

Comptroller-General—Johnson Hagood, of Barnwell;

Treasurer—S. L. Leaphart, of Richland;

Adjutant and Inspector-General—E. W. Moise, of Sumter.

The ticket represented the highest type of South Carolina's citizenship, and most of its members were particularly well qualified for the positions for which they had been named.

After the ticket had been completed, General Hampton was escorted into the convention by a committee. His appearance was greeted with prolonged applause. After it had subsided he made a stirring address, in which he said:

You are struggling for the highest stake for which a people ever contended, for you are striving to bring back to your prostrate State the inestimable blessings which can only follow orderly and regulated liberty under free and good government. We believe that these blessings can

---

[141]The writer was present as a spectator on the floor of the house on this memorable occasion.

[142]James Conner, the nominee for Attorney-General, had been a General in the Confederate Army, and was a leader of the "watch and wait" policy, in 1876. In a brief speech to the convention he accepted the nomination, and pledged the best that was in him to the success of the ticket. The nomination of Conner was indicative of the unity of spirit that, despite their differing views, prevailed among the Democrats.

only be secured by a complete change in the administration of our public affairs, National and State. * * * The platform which you have adopted here is so catholic in its spirit, so strong in its foundations, so broad in its construction, that every man in South Carolina who honestly desires reform can find room to stand upon it. With such a platform, where our citizens of all parties and all races can stand assured of equal rights and full protection, you can surely bring back to our distracted State the great blessings of good government. For myself, should I be elevated to the high position for which you have nominated me, my sole effort shall be to restore our State government to decency, to honesty, to economy, and to integrity. I shall be the Governor of the whole people, knowing no party.

Amid another outburst of cheering that followed Hampton's speech of acceptance, the convention adjourned *sine die*.[142a]

There was wild rejoicing in Columbia that night. Thousands, cheering, yelling in a pandemonium of joy, and in the glaring flames of a torchlight procession, moved down Main Street to the State House, where, from a stand erected in front of the building, speakers pledged themselves and their hearers to the support of the Democratic ticket. In every other part of the State the news of the nomination of a straight State ticket met with the same enthusiastic reception.

Wade Hampton, the hero of the most momentous event in South Carolina's history, was born March 28, 1818, on Hasel Street, in Charleston, within the sound of old St. Michael's chimes. He bore the full name of his father and his grandfather, from both of whom he also inherited his soldierly qualities. His great grandfather, who migrated from Virginia, and settled in Spartanburg County, South Carolina, was, together with his wife, his son Preston, and his infant grandchild, massacred by Indians. His son Wade escaped the massacre by reason of his absence from home. This Wade served in the Revolutionary War in Colonel William Washington's cavalry, and rose to the rank of lieutenant-colonel. He particularly distinguished himself at the battle of Eutaw Springs. He served as a Member of Congress in 1795-97, and again in 1803-05. In the War of 1812, he became a major-general and commanded an army of the United States on the Canadian border. He amassed a large fortune, having vast estates in Louisiana and Mississippi, as well as in South Carolina. The

---

[142a] As far as the author can ascertain the survivors (December 14, 1926) of the convention that nominated Hampton are: General C. Irvine Walker, Charleston; John R. Abney, Edgefield (now of New York City); Orlando Sheppard, Edgefield; Alexander McBee, Sr., Greenville; W. D. Hardy, Newberry; O. B. Riley, Orangeburg; Richard O'Neale, Jr., Richland.

son of the Revolutionary patriot, and father of the hero of 1876, usually known as Colonel Wade Hampton, was a lieutenant of dragoons in the War of 1812, and acted as aide and inspector-general on the staff of General Andrew Jackson at the battle of New Orleans. After the victory he rode on horseback the entire distance from New Orleans to Washington to bear the news to President Madison.

The third Wade Hampton was reared at Millwood, near Columbia, whose beautiful white pillars, twined with ivy, and surrounding a picturesque ruin, still stand as grim reminders of the fact that General W. T. Sherman once passed that way. He graduated from the South Carolina College (now the University of South Carolina) in 1836. Prior to the War of Secession, his large planting interests in Mississippi engaged his time and attention, and he spent most of his winters there. His family, surrounded by a host of slaves, lived like feudal barons. Born to the purple, Wade Hampton was an exponent of the highest type of the ante-bellum Southerner.

At the outbreak of the War of Secession, Hampton raised and organized the famous Hampton Legion, which he equipped largely at his own expense. His brilliant war record is another story, and one which would fill volumes. In 1863, General Lee commended Hampton's command in general orders, in which he used the highest terms of praise regarding it. In 1864, Hampton was made commander of the cavalry of Lee's army. Later, he was made Lieutenant-General. He was sent in 1865 to assist in the defense of the Carolinas, and in this way was not with his chief in the final struggle of the Confederacy.

As a result of the war, Hampton lost his wealth. While he was able to retain much of his lands in Mississippi, he was forced to live in very reduced circumstances.

Hampton possessed all the attributes that go to make up a leader as great in peace as in war. Exactly six feet in height, with massive head, broad shoulders and a stalwart frame, he was of commanding presence, and to this was added most prepossessing manners. He possessed unusual physical strength, and it is said that, on more than one occasion during the war, when engaged in single combat, he had cleft the skull of his adversary with a single stroke of his sabre and his strong right arm. A man of ability, character and education, he was an

orator of considerable power and had a sonorous voice, which
dominated his hearers in public assemblages.[143]

Hampton's most conspicuous traits of character were his
judgment, poise and tact in dealing with great emergencies.
There were times in 1876, when, a mad mob of his followers
surging around him ready for a bloody revolution if he but
said the word, he remained:

"Serene, and resolute, and still,
And calm, and self-possessed"—

allaying their tumultuous hearts by a mere wave of his hand.

Beginning in the spring, Governor Chamberlain had for some
months been making a personal canvass, speaking in a number
of counties. At some of the meetings Democrats had appeared
in large numbers, and insisted upon a division of time for their
speakers, and on account of their large numbers, usually got it.
Then the Democratic speakers, generally of the straightout element, would severely arraign the Governor. Some of the joint
meetings broke up in confusion, but without bloodshed. At
the meeting in Edgefield, early in August, after Chamberlain
had spoken, General Butler assailed him in very strong language for his course in the Hamburg affair, while General
Gary followed, scoring him roundly for his whole record in
South Carolina.[144]

The Republicans held their nominating convention in Columbia in September. Chamberlain was nominated for Governor
by a vote of 88 to 32 over his leading opponent, T. C. Dunn,
of Marlboro, then Comptroller-General. It appeared that
Chamberlain had made terms with the worst element of his
party to secure his renomination, for many of the most debauched Republicans, formerly his opponents, now supported
him; while those nominated with him made perhaps the most

[143]General Hampton was a famous hunter, particularly of big game.
[144]The Republican State platform denounced the tactics of Democrats at Republican campaign meetings. After condemning all forms of violence, intimidation, or
fraud, in elections and denying the charge that the Republican party wished to interfere with negroes who chose to vote the Democratic ticket, the platform went on
to say: "We protest against and denounce the practice now inaugurated by the
Democratic party in this State of attending Republican meetings, and, by show of
force and other forms of intimidation, disturbing such meetings, or taking part
therein without the consent or invitation of the party calling them."
   Chamberlain described the Democratic tactics at Republican meetings as "an
outrage upon free discussion, a mocking travesty of free speech, and a plain,
palpable, systematic attempt to deter Republicans from canvassing the State, and
to overawe and put in physical fear peaceful citizens assembled to discuss political
questions."—From letter to A. C. Haskell, Democratic State Chairman, October 4,
1876.

disreputable ticket that the Republicans had ever put forward in the State. The rest of the ticket was as follows:

Lieutenant-Governor—R. H. Gleaves;
Attorney-General—R. B. Elliott;
State Treasurer—F. L. Cardoza;
Secretary of State—H. E. Hayne;
Comptroller-General—T. C. Dunn;
State Superintendent of Education—John R. Tolbert;
Adjutant and Inspector-General—James Kennedy.

Of all the ticket the negro Elliott was, on account of his notoriously corrupt and immoral character, particularly offensive to the white people. He had for years been an opponent of Governor Chamberlain, and on many occasions had bitterly attacked him. In turn Chamberlain had excoriated Elliott as a man that everybody knew to be utterly devoid of character. When Elliott was a candidate for United States Senator, in 1872, Chamberlain had said that he (Chamberlain) would be willing to enter the race for the United States Senate if such a course were necessary to save the party from "negroism." While Elliott had retorted that he had in his possession a paper that would "consign Chamberlain to infamy."[145]

Chamberlain was now hard put to it to explain how his consent to be a candidate with such a running mate was not inconsistent with his previous open denunciation of the man, and with his outspoken stand for reform. In the course of the campaign, Chamberlain defended himself to the people of South Carolina by saying, "The causes of his [Elliott's] nomination were not his opposition to me, or to reform, but his admitted ability for the position, his long record of political service to the party, and a desire to conciliate an element which had been defeated in my renomination; and I am in no sense compromised or dishonored in my character as a Reformer by my association upon the same platform with Mr. Elliott."[146] A short time after the election Chamberlain admitted, however, to a friend in the North that he had made a grave mistake, and stated that he had resolved at the time of the convention to decline the renomination for Governor on the ground that he would not be a candidate on a ticket with Elliott. "I had

[145]When the nominees entered the hall to address the convention, they were headed by Chamberlain and Elliott, arm-in-arm.
[146]Letter to A. C. Haskell, Democratic State Chairman, October 4, 1876.

actually risen in my office to go into the [convention] hall for
this purpose," he wrote, "when I was met at the door by a
dozen or so of my supporters, who came to congratulate me on
the surrender of Elliott in seeking to stand on a ticket with me!
I was disarmed of my purpose, and relinquished it. It was a
mistake." [147]

There were many Democrats who, at the time of the State
Convention, had regarded nominations on a State Democratic
ticket as empty honors—some of the nominees holding that
view—but they began to look at the matter very differently a
few days after the convention had adjourned. They had not
counted upon the tremendous enthusiasm which Hampton's
name evoked. This enthusiasm spread almost in a moment,
throughout the length and breadth of South Carolina, from the
mountains to the sea, "from Sachem's head to Sumter's wall."

All difference of opinion among Democrats as to what course
to pursue were, after Hampton's nomination, buried forever.
Henceforward the Democrats stood as one man for the success
of the ticket. Strange as it may seem, in view of their past experience in political contests in the State, and of the seemingly
overwhelming obstacles ahead of them, the whites went forth
to battle hopeful of the result. Convinced of the righteousness
of their cause, they had an abiding faith in their ultimate
victory.

If anything had been needed to solidify the ranks of Democracy, it would have been furnished by the vicious ticket of the
Republicans. Chamberlain fell heavily in the estimation of the
white people for consenting to associate himself with such a
crowd. Upon even those who had believed him sincere in his
professions of reform was now forced the conviction that
Chamberlain had, by leaguing himself with deeply-dyed corruptionists, so bound himself to them that no reform could be
possibly expected from him.

Many of the more respectable Republicans were unwilling
to support so depraved a ticket, and they came over to the
Democratic side. Two of the earliest and most prominent de-
flections from Radical ranks were Judges T. J. Mackey and

[147]Letter to William Lloyd Garrison, the noted abolitionist, June 11, 1877.

Thompson H. Cook, both of whom became active for Hampton and accomplished much good work for him.[148]

---

[148]With Judge Mackey's career the reader has already been made familiar. Judge Cook, a native white Republican from Orangeburg County, was a lawyer of some experience, "a graduate of the State Military Academy and a well-meaning, good-natured man." After his election to the bench in 1872, he took no part in politics until he came out for Hampton and stumped the State for him, in 1876.— Reynolds, p. 229.

CHAPTER XVI

CAMPAIGN OF 1876—THE RED SHIRTS

Hampton and the other candidates on the State Democratic ticket conducted a whirlwind speech-making, county to county, canvass of the State—a canvass that was unique in the history of American politics. They addressed during the campaign at least one meeting at each county seat. Four accomplished speakers, besides Hampton, were on the State ticket—Simpson, Conner, Thompson and Moise—and they rendered valuable service on the stump. Volunteers from the ranks, many of them able orators, would, at one place or another, aid the State candidates by addressing the gatherings. Although it was the year of a Presidential campaign—with Samuel J. Tilden, of New York, the Democratic candidate for President, and Rutherford B. Hayes, of Ohio, the Republican candidate, and with issues of country-wide importance involved—little reference to national politics was made at these meetings, for the burning question of home rule overshadowed all else.

Other county meetings were, of course, held, and these led to precinct meetings in every nook and corner of the State. But the day that Hampton and his associates appeared at the county seat was for each county the great day of the campaign. It has passed into history as "Hampton Day."

By break of day the crowds began to gather at the county seat. Rifle clubs, which had been greatly increased in numbers, were there; and Red Shirt companies, which had evolved from the sabre clubs, and which took their name from their uniform —a red shirt usually of flannel, but sometimes of cambric, or calico, worn without a coat.[149] The women were all there to add to the success of the day. In fact, by time the hour set for the speaking had come, every Democrat in the county had joined the crowd; for was it not the day of all days of the campaign for every true white man to turn out to show his determination that on election day (November 7) civilization should be preserved in South Carolina!

The speaking was usually held in a grove on the edge of

---

[149]The adoption of the red shirt for a uniform is said to have been done in a spirit of defiance to the habitual "waving of the bloody (red) shirt" by the Radicals, North and South.

town, where a stand, hastily erected for the purpose, had been beautified by the women with bunting and flowers, twigs and branches. The procession from the centre of town to the grove was a spectacle to carry hope to the heart of every Democrat and despair to the heart of every Republican. The long line of Red Shirts, mounted and on foot, the shouting and yelling, the bands of music, the clatter of hoofs, and, above the din, the old time rebel yell, the hurrahing for Hampton or the hoarse strains from many voices of "We'll hang Dan Chamberlain on a sour apple tree," women and children following in carriages and waving banners and handkerchiefs, told a tale of enthusiasm gone wild.

But the effect of the county-to-county canvass can better be described by an abler pen: "Such delirium as they [the campaigners] aroused can be paralleled only by itself even in this delirious State. Their whole tour was a vast triumphal procession; at every depot they were received by a tremendous concourse of citizens and escorts of cavalry. Their meetings drew the whole white population, male and female (for the ladies turned out by tens of thousands to greet and listen to the heroic Hampton), for scores of miles around, and had to be held invariably in the open air. They were proceeded by processions of the rifle clubs, mounted and on foot, miles in length, marching amidst the strains of music and the booming of cannon; at night there were torchlight processions equally as imposing. The speakers aroused in thousands the memories of old, and called on their hearers to redeem the grand old State and restore it to its ancient place of honor in the Republic. The wildest cheering followed. The enthusiasm, as Confederate veterans pressed forward to wring their old General's hand, was indescribable. Large columns of mounted men escorted the canvassers from place to place while off the railroad. They were entertained at the houses of leading citizens, held receptions attended by all the wealth, intelligence, and brilliance of the community, and used all the vast social power they possessed to help on the work."[150]

"Hurrah for Hampton!" proved, during the campaign, as potent a slogan as that of "Remember the Maine!" which years later precipitated the war with Spain.

---

[150]"A South Carolinian" in the *Atlantic Monthly*, Vol. XXXIX, p. 183.

"As the election approached, the activity of the Democrats increased—so that for some little time before the day fixed by law the white people of South Carolina did practically nothing but work for Hampton and his ticket. Stores were actually closed, farms were left almost to take care of themselves, and everybody went to work for the redemption of the State. 'Hurrah for Hampton' went out all over South Carolina, and in that slogan there was a ring of resolution that made it veritably the death-knell of negro rule in this commonwealth. 'Hurrah for Hampton,' cried the Red Shirt from his horse or mule taken from the plough that he might join the procession. 'Hurrah for Hampton,' said the peace-making citizen who had just used his efforts to prevent a difficulty. 'Hurrah for Hampton,' was the jeer of a spirited man, when some arrogant negro Republican would pompously pass by. 'Hurrah for Hampton,' would (unconsciously) say a good Democrat as some white Republican happened to come along. 'Hurrah for Hampton' laughed the schoolboy, as he scampered along street or road. 'Hurrah for Hampton,' would say the swain as he bade his lady-love good night and joined some fellows in a search for a negro meeting, where they might divide time.

" 'Hurrah for Hampton' was the battle-cry of the white people of South Carolina in the fight to rid the State of negro rule !"[151]

This remarkable speech-making canvass began at Anderson, where the first "Hampton Day" was held on September 2. The attendance at this meeting was estimated at ten thousand. Some fifteen hundred Red Shirts were in line. As was the case at all subsequent meetings, a black face would be occasionally seen in a Red Shirt formation, conspicuous by its contrast with the many white faces surrounding it. The meetings wound up with the last "Hampton Day" at Columbia, on November 4, three days before the election.

The Republicans also had their public meetings; but their meetings were tame. The enthusiasm of the Democrats seemed to have dampened the ardor of the Republicans, for the speeches of their nominees showed that they were made half-heartedly. Governor Chamberlain's personal organ, the Columbia *Union-Herald*, endeavored to account for the lack of

---

[151]Reynolds, p. 361.

spirit at the Republican meetings by saying: "Public meetings are not necessary to arouse the Republicans, nor to inform them. On the day of election nine-tenths of them could be directed to cast their ballots at one poll, if necessary, and they would be there in spite of all the clubs in the country."[152]

The management of the Democratic campaign was under the care of the State Executive Committee, Colonel A. C. Haskell, Chairman, with headquarters in Columbia.[152a] The Executive Committee kept in close touch with Wade Hampton, whose cool, sound judgment at all times directed the course that the campaign should take.

The chief problems that confronted the Democrats from the outset of the campaign were: (1) how to restrain the intense feeling among the whites, aroused by the evils and horrors of Reconstruction, so that nothing would be done by them that would cause the United States Government to take over the affairs of the State—a calamity that would mean the continuance of the Republicans in power in the State; and (2) how to wipe out the huge majorities that the negroes had theretofore given the Republican tickets.

The Democratic organization was effected immediately after the nomination of Hampton, and it was soon functioning with such regularity that it resembled a military machine. The members of the Executive Committee who aided Hampton at the campaign headquarters in Columbia, his associates on the State ticket and the leaders in the several counties had been, with few exceptions, Confederate officers; while the rank and file of the party, with the exception of some of those who had become voters since the war, had been Confederate officers, or soldiers. The discipline learned in the war now served the Democrats in good stead. Orders issued by Hampton, or from

[152]The State Democratic Executive Committee endeavored to arrange with the Republicans for meetings where Hampton and Chamberlain might jointly discuss the issues of the campaign, and where provision would be made for preserving order, but the Republicans, remembering their experiences at joint meetings earlier in the year, were loath to agree. The insignificance of the Republican meetings which became manifest as the campaign progressed, gave the Democrats little incentive to continue their insistence by a show of force upon a division of time, even if the State Executive Committee would have approved of such a course.

[152a]Captain Richard O'Neale, a venerable and respected citizen of Columbia, who, as has been noted, is (December 14, 1926) one of the few survivors of the convention that nominated Hampton, is the sole survivor of the State Democratic Executive Committee of 1876. Captain O'Neal was also, during Reconstruction times, Captain of the Richland Volunteer Rifle Club.

his headquarters in Columbia, were, in turn, given by the leaders in the several counties to the rank and file. Obedience was the supreme duty, and with rare exceptions it was observed implicitly.[153]

The mediums through which the plans of the Democratic managers were carried out were the rifle clubs and the Red Shirt companies. Every county had a number of Red Shirt companies and many, if not most, of these companies were mounted.

In the dreadful times of Reconstruction, when no white man's life was safe, the whites had been compelled in self-defense to look upon firearms as necessary and proper. Like all habits that are desirable when necessary and undesirable when no longer necessary, the habit of carrying firearms continued after the necessity for doing so had passed, and has lasted to an unfortunate extent to this day in the South. This reprehensible condition is directly attributable to the evils of the Reconstruction era that was forced upon the South by the United States Government.

Although word had gone out from the Democratic leaders that violence was the last thing wanted, and should be resorted to only as a matter of self-defense, and, despite the discipline within the ranks, the great difficulty was in restraining the desperate characters among the whites, whom even experience in the Confederate Army had not taught the value of discipline, and the young bloods, whose enthusiasm was liable to carry them beyond the bounds of discretion The fact that the Republican leaders naturally wanted race troubles, added to the difficulty of the situation. That no clashes of a serious nature occurred for which the whites were responsible is a tribute to the wise counsel of Hampton and his lieutenants and the confidence held in them, and it is also a tribute to the courage, the sobermindedness and the good judgment of the masses of the white people.

To wipe out the Republican majority three methods were adopted. One was to persuade negroes to vote the Democratic ticket. Not only was the black man pleaded with individually by the whites, whenever opportunity occurred, but strenuous efforts were made at all public meetings to win negroes over to

---

[153]W. W. Ball, A Boy's Recollection of the Red Shirt Campaign, p. 21.

the Democratic party. Hampton believed thoroughly in his influence over the negroes, and much of his talk from the stump was directed to them. He always assured them that they would receive equal justice with the whites, "as soon as the power passes into the hands of the Democratic party here, which shall come to pass as surely as the sun goes down on November 7." But the negroes had had their minds so poisoned against the whites, first by the Freedmen's Bureau and the Loyal League, and afterwards by their leaders during Reconstruction—a condition which was rendered worse by their hostile attitude towards the Democratic members of their own race—that it is not probable that any considerable number of them were converted to the point of actually voting the Democratic ticket.

Another method of decreasing the Republican majority was to persuade, through the influence of some inducement, negroes who would not consent to vote the Democratic ticket to stay away from the polls altogether. It is probable that this plan, which was sometimes reinforced by the fear of loss of employment, did more to reduce the Republican vote than the first plan.

But the most effective method of all was one that the Republicans designated as "intimidation," and which unfriendly Northern historians have continued so to characterize it. As a rule, however, there was no actual violence, but only such manifestation of it as was consistent with keeping within the strict limits of the law.

Unexpectedly, and without apparent reason, mounted Red Shirts would appear on the streets of a town, or on the roads, firing pistols in the air, and making the welkin ring with their clamor.[154] The noise and tumult was well calculated greatly to exaggerate in the negro's mind the numbers of the mounted Red Shirts and to strike terror into his heart. The tactics of the mounted Red Shirts accomplished more for the successful outcome than probably any other phase of the campaign. When they were around, Republicans, carpetbaggers, scalawags and negroes, made themselves scarce, and the uncertainty as to when these grim, determined men with flaming shirts and on sweating horses might reappear had considerable effect in keeping the negroes quiet, and, above all, in hindering the efforts of their leaders to incite them to acts of violence.

[154]Ball, p. 17.

Of course, the whites transcended the strict limits of the law at times, even to the point of taking life. It is not to be expected that, in such a state of high tension, this "touch and go" policy could at all times be kept within the bounds of the law. The wonder is that, with the provocation they had, the transgressions of the whites were not more numerous.

It is well also to state here, that, in the campaign of 1876, the intimidation practiced upon negro Democrats by members of their own race far exceeded, both in its severity and in the number who were engaged in it, the intimidation of Republican negroes by the whites. A negro who announced his intention of voting for Hampton was turned out of his church and was ostracized and villified by his acquaintances in black, the women leading in the persecution. Often he was brutally assaulted and sometimes he was put to death. The Republican politicians and newspapers of the State said nothing about intimidation of negroes by negroes, but they raised, for the effect it would have upon the rest of the country and the Federal Government especially, a great outcry against intimidation of negroes by whites. Radicals at the North took up the outcry and echoed it.[155]

The women of South Carolina, as in all great crises of her history, did their part during the campaign. At every stage of it they encouraged and sustained the men, urging them to keep up the contest to the last and praying for their success. Their nimble fingers stitched the red shirts and they fed every Democrat who, in passing their house, might be hungry. Sometimes a woman would provide dinner for a whole company of Red Shirts. The strain upon the women from the dangers of the struggle cannot be overstated. Always hanging over them was the menace of a negro uprising. In rural sections, where there were few whites and many negroes, the tension was particularly severe. Often all the men on a place would be gone on a Red Shirt ride; and the half-grown boys would be gone, too, for many boys nearing manhood donned red shirts and proudly rode away, determined to be as vociferous in the "Red Shirt demonstration" as were their fathers and their older

---

[155]The use of the word "bulldoze" in the sense of intimidating, that has crept into our speech, began in the Reconstruction era. The word, strictly speaking, means to chastise with a bull-whip, to cowhide. Northern denunciators of the South during Reconstruction spoke of the alleged acts of intimidation of negroes by Southern whites as "bulldozing" methods—thence the word has come to be used in the United States to refer to intimidation or coercion of any kind.

brothers. The women would be left with their dauntless courage, and perhaps, a stripling of a boy as their only protection; yet, they never faltered. They made up for not having then the right to vote by their fortitude and their enthusiasm.

Wade Hampton was of a kindly, generous nature that shrunk from violence except when necessity absolutely demanded it; and his judgment never erred as to when the necessity had arisen. He realized no more fully than did many others the dangers and difficulties that beset the Democrats; yet there was probably no other man in the State whose temperament would have held him so utterly free from the possibility of being swayed, by the woes of his people, to indiscreet action, or who would have inspired in all men a confidence that made them so unhesitatingly follow him. Without Hampton there would probably have been much bloodshed and all its attending calamities; with Hampton "the hour and the man met." He was the leader to guide straightout Democracy through tortuous paths to success.

In according Wade Hampton so much credit for what was accomplished, it is neither with the desire nor the intention of taking from any other man the part which he performed in the redemption of South Carolina. Had it not been for the efficient and faithful help of his official and volunteer aides, had it not been for the intelligent and courageous support of the people, Hampton would have been powerless to achieve a victory.

CHAPTER XVII

RIOTS DURING THE CAMPAIGN—DISBANDING THE RIFLE CLUBS

In spite of the efforts of the Democratic leaders, it was impossible, on account of the ugly mood of the negroes, for the campaign to proceed to the end without disorder. If the negroes had been left free from evil influences it is probable that no trouble of consequence would have occurred; for the well-known readiness of the white race to defend itself, at all times, which the negroes understood and appreciated, was having a good effect. But the Republican leaders, North as well as South, were resolved that there should be violence in South Carolina, so as to furnish justification for interference on the part of the United States government.

The Republicans in the North had become very anxious about the election for President. Every indication pointed to a close contest, with the chances in favor of Tilden, the Democratic nominee, and it was a matter of great concern to the Northern Republicans that the electoral vote of the three Southern states still under carpetbag domination[156] be made safe for Hayes. Race riots would serve the double purpose of placing the election in these states in charge of the national government, and of furnishing occasion for strengthening the Hayes' following in the North by further "waving of the bloody shirt."

The Republican negroes in South Carolina, especially in the low country, where their great predominance of numbers inspired them with overconfidence, assumed a very aggressive attitude toward the whites, and towards the Democrats of their own race. Negroes, estimated to the number of 40,000, had been secretly furnished with rifles by the State. This had a tendency to increase the enrollment in the rifle clubs, while their equipment was considerably improved. Mounted Red Shirts, as a deterrent to turbulent negroes, patrolled the roads at night. In sparsely settled communities, where there were neither rifle clubs nor Red Shirt organizations, the few white men would band themselves together

---

[156]South Carolina, Florida and Louisiana.

for the protection of their families. With both of the opposing parties thus constituting armed camps, the tension was extreme. Still, Hampton and their other leaders, were, as a rule, able to hold the white men in check.

The first serious outbreak of the campaign occurred in Charleston early in September, occasioned by the attempt of a negro mob to attack two Democratic negroes, whom a small party of whites were protecting. The whites, greatly outnumbered, had a hard time of it trying to hold off the frenzied negroes. For more than an hour the mob held possession of the streets, discharging their firearms promiscously, and smashing windows. One white man was killed and seven were wounded. Five negroes were wounded, three of whom were members of the police force which had endeavored to quell the riot. Disorders followed in other parts of the city, but they were controlled by the rifle clubs, which had been called to the assistance of the police. Chamberlain said subsequently that "the most trustworthy information seems to fix the responsibility for causing the riot upon the Republicans."

One of the most serious race riots occurred in the middle of September at Ellenton, a town in Aiken County, near the Barnwell line. The riot started from an effort to arrest two negroes, who, while attempting a burglary, had brutally beaten a white woman occupying the residence which they had entered. Negroes from miles around suddenly appeared in large numbers, and heavily armed. Whites from adjacent sections of Aiken and Barnwell Counties quickly flew to arms. The race clash that spread over a wide range of the two counties lasted for two days. The whites had two killed and eight wounded; and the negroes fifteen killed and two wounded. A company of negro militia took a prominent part in the riot, and during its progress tore up part of a railroad track near Ellenton and wrecked a train. The riot was finally quelled by a company of United States soldiers which was sent to the scene at the request of Governor Chamberlain. The Ellenton riot was non-political in its origin, and would not have assumed such proportions had it not been for the race hatred with which the negroes had been inspired by their leaders.

What was known as the "Cainhoy Massacre" occurred near the middle of October at Cainhoy, in Charleston County, in the "black belt," where the negroes outnumbered the whites ten to one. A joint meeting by the Democrats and Republicans had been arranged, with an agreement that neither side should take their rifles to the meeting. The negro, Martin R. Delany, was to be one of the speakers for the Democrats. The meeting had not progressed far when the negroes, most of whom were particularly hostile to the whites, began a row. The negroes rushed for their rifles, which they had concealed nearby, and fired upon the few white men who were present. The whites, accompanied by Delany, took refuge in a brick house adjoining the church. The negroes made an assault upon the house, but everyone succeeded in escaping from it except an old white man, who was knocked down and beaten to death, his assailants discharging a load of buckshot into his prostrate body. In this riot six white men were killed and sixteen wounded, some very seriously. Only one negro was killed. After the riot white men from Charleston flocked to Cainhoy, but further trouble was averted by the arrival of United States soldiers, whom Governor Chamberlain, at the suggestion of a committee of white citizens, had requested the commander of United States forces in the State to send to the scene of the disturbance.

Riots of lesser consequences occurred in every part of the State, and in almost every instance the negroes were clearly the aggressors. More than three hundred white citizens of Aiken and Barnwell Counties, suspected of participation in the Ellenton riot, were arrested by the United States authorities on a charge of having violated the "Force Bills." White citzens of Edgefield, Marion and Pickens Counties, where there had been disturbances, were also arrested. None of the accused were ever tried, with the exception of a few of those from Aiken County, and in their cases the juries could not agree. "Honest John" Patterson afterwards boasted that 700 Democrats, in all had been arrested in the State during the campaign.[157]

While none of the responsibility for the incitement of the negroes to violence can be directly traced to Governor Chamberlain certain it is that he lost no time in making political capital for himself out of the disorders. Now that he had no hope of gaining the support of any portion of the white

[157]Edward L. Wells, Hampton and Reconstruction, p. 137.

voters in his race for re-election, he seemed no longer to prize the good opinion of the respectable people of the State. Availing himself of the opportunity afforded by the Ellenton riot, he wrote to President Grant, reminding him that, after the Hamburg riot, the President had promised him assistance. In his letter to the President, Chamberlain stated that the time had come when additional troops were most needed in South Carolina.[158] He also told the President that rifle clubs were appearing all over the State and that he had knowledge that these clubs numbered at least 213 with a membership of 13,-000.[159] President Grant, however, was visiting in California and Chamberlain's letter had to await his return.

But Chamberlain himself did not wait to take action. On October 7 he issued a proclamation in which he alleged that unlawful combinations of persons existed in the Counties of Barnwell and Aiken, and that illegal organizations known as rifle clubs existed in all the counties of the State;[160] that these rifle clubs, strictly forbidden by the laws of the State, were engaged in promoting unlawful objects and committing acts of violence. The Governor, therefore, called upon the lawless assemblages in Aiken and Barnwell Counties to disperse. He further forbade the existence of all rifle clubs, and ordered them and all similar organizations not forming a part of the militia of the State forthwith to disband. The proclamation closed with a promise of martial law in the event that it was disobeyed.

The white people were indignant at Chamberlain's proclamation. Knowing that the negroes were almost entirely to blame for the disturbances, and that, if they had been properly controlled by their leaders, the policy of forbearance on the part of the whites would have assured peace, they regarded Chamberlain's proclamation as an infamous libel on the State. On

---

[158]The authority under which the Republican Legislatures and Republican Governors of South Carolina so often asked the aid of Federal troops is found in Article IV, Section 4, of the Constitution of the United States, which reads: "The United States shall protect each of them [the several states] against invasion; and, on application of the Legislature or of the Executive (when the Legislature cannot be convened) against domestic violence."

[159]In the summer of 1876, the rifle clubs throughout the State formed a general organization under the following officers: General James Conner, Commander; Major Theodore G. Barker, Commander of the Lower Division, and Col. Samuel B. Pickens, Commander of the Upper Division—Walker, p. 53.

[160]In the earlier part of his administration, Chamberlain had tacitly accepted the existence of the few rifle clubs then organized for professedly social purposes; but the hundreds that had been organized since the opening of the campaign of 1876 with a purpose so clearly other than social, he viewed in a different light.

the day it was issued, the State Democratic Executive Committee replied to it in an address to the people of the United States that they might have a true statement of the condition of affairs in South Carolina. The address first cited the fact that the Governor, in a time of profound peace, when the courts were open and the civil law could be enforced, had threatened martial law. In the opinion of the committee the Governor's "false and libelous" statements, and his "disregard of law and fact" were due to his determination to save himself, by extreme measures, from the defeat facing him. The riot at Ellenton, which was the alleged provocation for the proclamation, the committee showed was non-political and the negroes were to blame for it. Furthermore, peace and quiet had long since prevailed in the parts of Aiken and Barnwell Counties affected by the riot. The committee then called attention to the fact that the Republicans had held meetings whenever and wherever they wished, without one act of violence by whites having occurred. Accompanying the address were statements from most of the Supreme Court and Circuit Court Judges of the State, who had been elected by the Republicans, and the Sheriffs of Aiken and Barnwell Counties, all of which confirmed the assertion of the State Committee that there was no violence or any other lawlessness that the civil courts could not take care of, nor any signs of a disposition to resist the civil law. The address concluded:

"We assert earnestly, with a full sense of our responsibility, that no condition of things exists in this State which justifies so extraordinary a proceeding on the part of Governor Chamberlain. Its sole object is to irritate and provoke collisions which may be the excuse for an appeal to the administration of the United States to garrison the State. We shall counsel our people to preserve the peace, observe the laws and calmly await the day of their deliverance from this wanton despotism. To the people of the United States we submit our wrongs, confidently relying on their wisdom and justice to rebuke this daring attempt to regulate the ballot by the bayonet and crush the liberties of a people."

The Governor, in turn, issued on October 9, an address to the people of the United States, in which after promising to make public all evidence in his hands and in the hands of the

United States District Attorney, to show the "atrocity" of the "lawlessness, terrorism and violence" in the State, added: "I pledge myself to the country to prove a condition of affairs in this State, produced by the Democratic party, more disgraceful than any statement yet made by me, and I shall not stay my hand until punishment overtakes its guilty authors. My only offense is too great caution in obtaining evidence, and too great delay in exercising my utmost powers to protect our citizens."

CHAPTER XVIII

GRANT BACKS UP CHAMBERLAIN

President Grant, immediately upon his return from California, took up the matter of Chamberlain's request for assistance. The determination of the partisan Republican administration at Washington to help Chamberlain, whether by proper or improper means, is made clear by the fact that it sent additional United States troops to South Carolina, knowing that such action was not necessary to preserve the peace. Grant not only accepted the word of Chamberlain against the testimony of prominent citizens of the State, of both political parties, but he accepted it in preference to the statement of the officer whom he himself had sent to South Carolina to command the United States troops already stationed there.

On October 13, General W. T. Sherman, commanding the United States army, sent the following telegram to General T. H. Ruger, commanding the troops in South Carolina:

Headquarters of the Army
Washington, October 14, 1876
To General Ruger, Columbia, S. C.:
We are all back from California. If you want anything say so. I want all measures to originate with you. Get along with the minimum force necessary, but you shall have all we can give if you need them.
W. T. SHERMAN,
General.

Two days later General Sherman received from General Ruger this telegram in reply:

Columbia, S. C., October 16, 1876
To Gen. W. T. Sherman, Washington, D. C.:
Think I have troops sufficient unless circumstances change. Have nineteen companies in State now in stations of one to four companies. Have some companies still in reserve. No special disorder has occurred since Ellenton riot last month. If I need more troops I will ask for them. I shall be here to-day.

RUGER

Notwithstanding General Sherman's assertion that no more troops than were needed should be sent to South Carolina, and that General Ruger should be the judge of when the necessity for additional troops had arisen; notwithstanding General Ruger's positive statement that no more troops were needed because peace prevailed in the State, President Grant, on the day following the receipt of General Ruger's telegram (October 17) issued a proclamation denouncing the rifle clubs in South Carolina which, he charged, "ride up and down by day and night in arms, murdering some peaceable citizens and intimidating others," and commanding the clubs, as insurgents, to disband.

Then he ordered all the available troops in the military district of the Atlantic to be transferred to South Carolina. The Secretary of War directed General Sherman to instruct General Ruger "to station his troops in such localities that they may be most speedily and effectually used, in case of resistance to the authority of the United States," and added:

It is hoped that a collision may thus be avoided, but you will instruct General Ruger to let it be known that it is the fixed purpose of the Government to carry out fully the spirit of the proclamation, and to sustain it by the military force of the General Government, supplemented, if necessary, by the militia of the various States.

The people of South Carolina were again indignant. They deeply resented that they should be treated in such manner, first by the government of their State, and then by the government of their nation, but there was no disposition to disobey either proclamation. Hampton, to make sure that resistance would not be made, telegraphed to prominent citizens of Aiken and Barnwell:

Urge our people to submit peaceably to martial law. I will see and consult with them.

The State Democratic Committee issued another appeal—this time "To the people of the State of South Carolina who desire honest government, without regard to political party or race," and in protest against President Grant's proclamation. The Committee arraigned Governor Chamberlain in unmeasured terms for his false statements to the President and warned the other States of the Union that the " 'domination of our election by the bayonet and by soldiers as the irresistible instrument of a revolutionary local despotism,' if successful, will become the precedent before which the whole fabric of American liberty will fall, and will be applied to other States just as soon as party exigencies require it."

The State Committee exhorted the people "to yield full and entire obedience to the President's proclamation," and explained the existence of the rifle clubs in these telling phrases:

"We know that the clubs called 'rifle clubs' are associations formed for home protection; that they are not combinations as charged by the Governor of this State; that there are but few that have arms or ammunition; that those which have been so equipped were so done with the sanction and sometimes with the aid of the Governor, and have been recognized by him as useful and appropriate bodies, and not one of them has been accused of disorder. . . . We know that their necessity was occasioned by the reckless distribution of arms and ammunition among the colored people by the State officials. . . . We know that the politicians who are the authors of all our evils are teaching among the colored race the use of the rifle and the torch; we know that our homes are in peril, and that our women and children are exposed to the horrors of ruthless butchery and barbarity; but, nevertheless, we advise and command, so far as our authority goes, that every such 'rifle club' against which the misrepresentations of the Governor of the State are aimed be forthwith disbanded, and that the members thereof be held in future only by those ties of humanity which bind all good men together; that the name of the club be abandoned, and the officers cease to exercise their powers. This is said with the express declaration that these clubs are not associated with or subject to our political control."[161]

The mandates of the Governor and of the President were obeyed to the extent that the rifle clubs ostensibly disbanded, and no longer appeared in public on parades or drills. They retained their arms, however, which were their own property, and as some well-disciplined force of white men was necessary for protection, they did not entirely terminate their organization. They would have fallen back into line at a drum beat. The Richland Rifle Club of Columbia stretched a streamer across Main Street from their armory to the opposite building, upon which was emblazoned in large letters the words, "Disbanded, but solid for Hampton."[162]

---

[161]The appeal made further reply to the President's proclamation as follows: "We cannot 'disperse,' because we are not banded together—we cannot 'retire to our homes,' because we are already there."

[162]Governor Chamberlain demanded of the Richland Rifle Club the rifles for which they had paid a consideration to an official of the State government during Moses' administration. This demand elicited the following reply from the President of the Club:

"I have the honor to state that the arms are now in the hands of the gentlemen formerly composing the Club. The Club having been disbanded, I will use all possible *personal* diligence in collecting the arms and returning them as directed." These rifles were never turned in. Some of the surviving members of the Club have theirs to this day.

The only real effect President Grant's proclamation had was to increase the resentment on the part of the whites in the State against him, and more especially against Governor Chamberlain, who gave the false information on which the President's proclamation was based.

Heavy reinforcements of Federal troops were sent into the prostrate State. The total number on election day was at least 5,000. With the arrival of the additional Federal soldiers, the negroes became more violent and aggressive, particularly in the black counties; while their persecution of negro Democrats became brutal in the extreme. It was noted everywhere that in their bitter hatred and denunciation of the whites and the negro Democrats the negro women were even more violent than the men. Both races (particularly the whites who had no military equipment) began to receive heavy importations of arms and ammunition, which, in the case of the whites, were packed as hardware, groceries, etc., to escape detection.

At the suggestion of the State Democratic Committee that the ministers of the gospel "open the churches for service and lead us in the prayer unto Almighty God that justice, peace and prosperity, mercy and truth, with fellowship and good feeling to all men, may come back and prevail among our long suffering and much disturbed people," religious services were held in all the churches of the State on October 28, a few days before the election.

The county-to-county canvass of the State Democratic candidates had continued undeterred by the disturbances throughout the State. In Charleston, late in October, was held one of the largest and most enthusiastic meetings of the campaign. A parade of ten thousand men, many of them Red Shirts, passed through streets bedecked with flags and banners. At the head of the procession were General Hampton and General (then Senator) John B. Gordon, of Georgia. General Gordon had been in the State for some time, giving inestimable aid to her people in their struggle for a white man's government. On the occasion of the Charleston campaign meeting he received an ovation which was second only to that accorded Wade Hampton.

The canvass ended with a monster meeting at Columbia on November 4. A great crowd gathered from every part of the

State to make this meeting a demonstration that would be a
fitting culmination to the stirring campaign. The enthusiasm
far exceeded anything that had gone before. With echoes
from the impassioned ring of orators, the boom of cannon
and the shouts of multitudes, the unique canvass of 1876 passed
into history.

CHAPTER XIX

Both Sides Claim the Election

At last, with the tension strained to the utmost, the day of the election arrived. At all the county seats, and at other places where trouble was apprehended, a detachment of United States soldiers had been stationed, while at every poll United States supervisors of election, equally divided between the two politicial parties, kept watch on affairs. Each poll had three managers—two Republicans and one Democrat.

The white voters, besides casting their ballots, busied themselves in seeing to it that the negro Democrats voted without interference from those of their own race. Demonstrations for the purpose of impressing the Republican negroes continued throughout the day of election. In some places Red Shirts crowded around the polls, where the excitement which they created had the effect of deterring some of the more timid Republicans from approaching the ballot box. Most of the officers of the United States army had come to sympathize with the State in her desperate condition, and as long as there were neither open acts of violence, nor actual threats of it, they permitted the demonstrations of the Democrats to go unheeded. Notwithstanding the strain upon everyone, which had grown more and more severe as the campaign progressed, the final day passed in comparative quiet, except in the low country where the negroes, on account of their numbers, had things very much their own way. In that section gangs of negro toughs, armed with rifles and pistols, knives and clubs, went from poll to poll, and by driving negro Democrats away, prevented many of them from voting. Attempts of the few white men around to prevent the overawing of Democratic negroes caused some clashes between the races, but even then there was remarkably little bloodshed.

Instead of the tension decreasing, however, it increased with the passing of election day, for the result was in doubt. The returns, which came in very slowly, made it evident from the first that the election was close. On the morning after the election the Republicans seemed to have carried the State for both the national and the State tickets. On November 17, however, it was unofficially stated that Hampton had been elected by a majority of 1,323. All the while both sides claimed the victory and each side accused the other of gross fraud and intimidation.

The National election was also very close; in fact, its result depended upon the electoral votes of the States which were still dominated by the carpetbaggers—South Carolina, Louisiana and Florida—and the votes of each of these States were claimed for both Tilden and Hayes. The anxiety of the Northern Republicans to hold for Hayes the electoral vote of South Carolina was seen in the increased aggressiveness of the negroes after election day.[163]

The slowness with which the returns were received and the many conflicting reports which were in circulation regarding them—the charges and counter-charges of fraud and intimidation, together with the increased insolence of the negroes—all combined to cause feeling throughout the State to rise to boiling point. Serious rioting occurred in Charleston, the trouble starting there on the day after the election. On the day following—November 9—the negroes broke away from all restraint. At the lower end of Broad Street, the busiest part of the city and at the busiest hour of the day, a negro policeman fired his pistol twice at some fifty white men who were watching a bulletin board for belated election returns. The shots injured no one, but they seemed to have been the signal for the appearance of a mob of negroes. The whites were greatly outnumbered at first but they held their ground valiantly, and after a considerable time, and with great difficulty, drove off their assailants. The casualties among the whites was one killed—Ellicot H. Walter, a peaceably disposed young man, who was shot dead in his tracks—and twelve wounded. The negroes had one killed and eleven wounded. Although the riot occurred almost within a stone's throw of police headquarters, a detachment of police arrived on the scene only when the negroes had been driven away. Later, a second mob of negroes collected in another part of the city, but United States troops, which now appeared, cleared the streets of all riotous negroes.

The people of Charleston were in little mood to submit to

---

[163]Wells, p. 145.

such outrageous assaults from negroes. Some 500 whites, fully
armed, had rushed to Broad Street at the time of the riot,
while the rifle clubs had assembled in their armories. By
this time, however, cooler heads had taken charge. Conservative leaders advised those who would make reprisals upon the
negroes that Hampton wished further trouble to be avoided
because of its probable effect upon the election returns, and a
wish of Hampton was sufficient to quiet the angriest heart.

During the riot, the rifle clubs, which, it will be remembered
had been disbanded by President Grant, had offered their services to General Hunt, who commanded the United States troops
in Charleston. Their services having been accepted, they acted
in conjunction with the soldiers in clearing the streets. The
negroes had always believed that the United States soldiers
would help them keep the white people underfoot. The sight,
therefore, of the troops fraternizing with the rifle clubs—
the objects of the negroes' special dread and hatred—had an
amazing effect in bringing most of them to their senses. This
tactful act of General Hunt cost him his command in Charleston, however; for a leading carpetbagger of that city complained of him to Washington, and the gallant officer was transferred to a station outside the State.[164]

For some days following the riot there were still signs of
unrest among the negroes of Charleston, and they beat up and
shot all white men and negro Democrats who had the temerity
to appear upon the streets alone. The Republican Mayor,
George I. Cunningham, confessed his inability to cope with the
situation, and the police had shown that they were powerless
to protect life and property. Upon the advice of General
Hampton, and with the consent of the Mayor, a committee of
leading white citizens requested the United States troops to
patrol the city. The Mayor also agreed, at the suggestion of
the citizens' committee, that if another outbreak should occur,
he would call on General James Conner, then in command of
the rifle clubs, to assist the troops in maintaining order.

Other parts of the State also suffered greatly. The torch,
which had proved a standing menace throughout the period of

---

[164]Wells, 145, 146; F. A. Porcher's Last Chapter of Reconstruction in South
Carolina, published in the Southern Historical Society papers, Vol. XII, p. 179.
Professor Porcher says: "General Hunt . . . was instantly reported to the
President at Washington, and was almost as instantly sent elsewhere on duty."

Reconstruction, especially in the country, now increased its deadly work; and it was not uncommon at night to see the heavens lit up in several directions, indicating that the houses or barns of the whites were falling before the vengeance of their political enemies.

The complete election returns, when they finally reached the State Board of Canvassers at Columbia, indicated that the Democrats had elected the Governor, Lieutenant-Governor, Secretary of State, Attorney-General and Comptroller-General; and that the Republicans had elected the State Treasurer, State Superintendent of Education and Adjutant and Inspector-General. The Republican ticket for Presidential electors appeared to have won by a majority of 1,100, while the Democrats seemed to have elected two out of five Congressmen and five out of eight Solicitors. The returns gave seats in the House of Representatives of the State to sixty-four Democrats and sixty Republicans. Of the places in the State Senate filled at this election the Democrats won twelve and the Republicans six. Since the hold-over Senators numbered three Democrats and twelve Republicans, the returns gave the Democrats a majority of one in the Legislature on joint ballot.

The rejoicing among the Democrats, when the returns showed that they had been successful, cannot be described. General Hampton issued the following address:

To the People of the State:
In offering to our people my heartfelt congratulations and gratitude for the grand victory they have won, I venture to beg them to prove themselves worthy of it by a continued observance of good order and a rigid preservation of peace. Let us show that we seek only the restoration of good government, the return of prosperity and the establishment of harmony to the whole people of our State.
In the hour of victory we should be magnanimous, and we should strive to forget the animosities of the contest by recalling the grand results of our success. Prescribing none for the difference of opinion, regarding none as enemies, save such as are inimical to law and order, let us all unite in the patriotic work of redeeming the State. By such conduct we can not only bring about good feeling among all classes, but can most surely reap the best fruits of victory.

The Republican managers, including Chamberlain, denying the correctness of the returns, still claimed the election. They declared that the figures of the returns had been brought about by juggling, fraud and intimidation on the part of the Democrats. The charge was met by the Democrats with the claim that the grossest fraud and intimidation had been practiced by the Republicans. The whites had no thought of allowing the Republicans to take the election from them. Desperate but determined they saw further trouble staring them in the face.

Without doubt fraud was committed by Democrats at many places in the State and the extent to which they practiced intimidation has already been shown. But the Republicans of South Carolina were the last who should have complained. During all the years of Reconstruction and particularly in the sections of the State where they were in a great majority, the negroes, under the guidance of their designing leaders, had practiced the most brutal forms of intimidation and had perpetrated all kinds of frauds at the ballot box. Moreover, their intention of continuing their fraudulent practices in the election of 1876 was discovered and the Democrats prepared to checkmate them. For instance, in Charleston County, where the negroes outnumbered the whites, they committed, in 1876, the most flagrant frauds at the ballot box to swell their majority to more than 6,000 votes.

In the counties where the whites predominated, or were relatively strong in numbers, the order of things was reversed. It was charged that in Edgefield "repeating" and other forms of fraud were freely indulged in by Democrats, and that many Georgians crossed the Savannah River to that county to vote the Democratic ticket.

Fortunately Wade Hampton's own words may be cited: "I believe that there was fraud in the election of that year [1876] . . . . The Republicans in Charleston had 10,000 tissue ballots printed and the Democrats hearing of it printed a large batch themselves and used them. It was clearly demonstrated that the Republicans printed them first and the Democrats followed the lead."[165]

Without intention to justify improper methods, it is well to consider, in view of the desperate condition to which the State had been reduced, and in view of the fact that ordinary methods

[165]From an interview with Hampton published in the Boston *Herald*, November 28, 1879, and republished in the Columbia *Register*, December 13, 1879.
   Taylor (negro Republican author) says, p. 250: "There can be little doubt that fraud and intimidation were resorted to by both parties. . . . With a few exceptions the vote of every county was protested to the Board of State Canvassers."

for her redemption would not have availed, whether there was
not some palliation for the resort to methods which would never
be warranted except as a last resort in time of revolution.[166]

---

[166]S. S. ("Sunset") Cox, long a distinguished member of Congress from Ohio
and New York, says in his Three Decades of Federal Legislation: "The knaves
and their sympathizers, North and South, complain that the taxpayers, men of
character and intelligence, in South Carolina, and other States, finally overthrew,
by violent and unfair means, the reign of scoundrelism, enthroned by ignorance.
If ever revolutionary methods were justifiable for the overthrow of tyranny and
robbery, assuredly the carpetbag domination in South Carolina called for it.
Only scoundrels and hypocrites will pretend to deplore the result."

CHAPTER XX

United States Soldiers in the State House

The State Board of Canvassers, composed of five State officials, met in Columbia the week following the election for the purpose of canvassing the returns sent in by the county boards of canvassers.

The statute relating to the State Board of Canvassers required that the Board, after canvassing the returns, should declare what persons were elected, and should issue certificates of election accordingly. In case of a contest for the Governorship, however, the statute provided that the Legislature, if each House, acting separately, decided it was advisable to do so, should determine who had been elected to that office.

Soon after convening, the Board announced that, since the statute made the Legislature the final judge in the election of Governor, it would not go behind the returns—that is, that it would not investigate the question of their correctness—in the case of the Governor and the Lieutenant-Governor (for the case of the Governor carried with it the Lieutenant-Governor). At the same time the Board announced that the statute imposed upon it the duty of examining into the correctness of the returns in the election of members of the Legislature, just as in the election for all other officials except Governor and Lieutenant-Governor.

The scheme of the Republicans was plain. As all the members of the State Board of Canvassers were Republicans and intense partisans of Chamberlain, it would be an easy matter for them to find, in the charges of fraud and intimidation alleged to have been committed by the Democrats, a pretext to throw out a sufficient number of the returns in cases where Democrats had been elected to the House of Representatives to give control of that body to the Republicans. With the Senate already Republican the consent of each House, as required by law, could be obtained for throwing out votes that gave Hampton a majority on the face of the returns and declaring Chamberlain the legally elected Governor.

The Democrats had all along contended that the statute could not give the State Board of Canvassers power to go behind the returns in the election of members of the Legislature, for to do so would be unconstitutional since the State Constitution declared that "each house shall judge of the election returns and qualifications of its own members." Therefore, further contended the Democrats, the duty of the Board in the case of the Legislature was purely ministerial—that is, the Board should merely certify to the returns as it found them. Under this procedure the Democrats, having a majority of the House, would organize that body, accept the returns as correct, and declare Hampton elected. The Republican State Supreme Court sustained the Democrats in their contentions. Upon the application of Colonel A. C. Haskell, as chairman of the State Democratic Executive Committee, the Court issued a writ of mandamus, commanding the State Board of Canvassers to declare elected as Senators and Representatives all persons whom the returns showed to have received the highest number of votes.[167]

When the State Board of Canvassers heard of the action of the Supreme Court, it hurried forward with its scheme. The Board issued certificates of election to all persons who were shown to be elected to the Legislature by the returns, except those from Edgefield and Laurens Counties, where the returns gave the Democrats large majorities. The Board, on the ground of fraud and intimidation, threw out the returns from these two counties entirely, and declared that there had been no election for the eight seats in the House from Edgefield and Laurens Counties. By this action the Board thought to give the House to the Republicans, for, if their actions should be sustained, the vote of that body would be, Republican, 59; Democratic, 57. The action of the Board also gave the vote of

---

[167]The State offices, besides those of Governor and the Lieutenant-Governor, were claimed by both sides. Under other circumstances the State Board of Examiners would have undoubtedly had, under the law, the right to examine into the correctness of the returns for these offices. In this election, however, three members of the Board, constituting a majority—Hayne, Cardoza and Dunn—were candidates for re-election, and it was impossible to separate the election in the case of one office from that of another, since they were all voted for on the same ticket. Therefore, the Democrats claimed that the Board was disqualified, since it is an admitted principle of law that one cannot sit as a judge in one's own cause. Colonel Haskell, as chairman of the State Democratic Executive Committee, carried the case of the State offices (other than Governor and Lieutenant-Governor) to the State Supreme Court at the same time that he carried the case of the Legislature, but the Court postponed its decision as to that case.

the State to Hayes. The Board then adjourned before it could be served with the Court's writ of mandamus.[168]

This defiance of the Supreme Court of the State by the Board of Canvassers not only aroused indignation in South Carolina and elsewhere in the South, but it met with much disapproval in the North. Many of the leading newspapers throughout the country strongly condemned the course of the Board.

General Hampton issued an appeal to the people urging them, in spite of the "high-handed outrage well calculated to arouse the indignation of a long-suffering people," to maintain the character of a law-abiding people which they had gained by their avoiding during the exciting campaign "even the semblance of a purpose to disturb the public peace or to transgress the law." He assured them that the "daring and revolutionary act of the Board can have no force whatever." "Your cause, and it is in the cause of constitutional government in this country," he said, "has been carried to the highest Court of the State, and we are willing to abide by its decision, feeling assured that this tribunal will see that the laws shall be enforced and justice succeed."

The State Supreme Court, its attention having been called to the unlawful action of the State Board of Canvassers, issued warrants for the arrest of all the members of the Board on the charge of contempt. There was some doubt whether the warrants would or could be served, but Colonel Haskell resolved the doubt by inducing Sheriff Dent, of Richland County, who was a Republican, to go with him at midnight to the homes of the members of the Board, where the Sheriff arrested them and lodged them in jail.

Judge Hugh L. Bond, of the United States Circuit Court, was in Columbia at the time the members of the Board were put under arrest. This Judge had already made himself particularly obnoxious to the white people of South Carolina by his biased course while presiding over the Ku Klux trials. Judge Bond, two days after the arrests were made, ordered the Sheriff of Richland County to bring the arrested officials before the United States Court. After hearing arguments in the case, Judge Bond released the prisoners from custody, on

---

[168]All the proceedings of the State Board of Canvassers were taken at the instance of Governor Chamberlain.

the ground that their arrests were illegal since they were made upon an action of the Board that involved duties imposed by the Constitution and laws of the United States (the counting of the votes for Presidential electors and for members of Congress).

The State Supreme Court having, by the action of the United States Court, failed in its mandate to the Board, but still holding that the Democrats claiming seats in the House from Edgefield and Laurens had been duly elected on the face of the returns, issued certificates of election to them.

As the day for the convening of the Legislature (November 28) approached, apprehension of serious trouble on account of the excitement over the unsettled political conditions was felt throughout the State, but the white people continued firm in their purpose to use every lawful means to frustrate the designs of the Republicans. Chamberlain applied for United States troops to be used in the State House and President Grant addressed the following letter to the Secretary of War:

Executive Mansion, November 26, 1876.

Hon. J. D. Cameron, Secretary of War.

Sir: D. H. Chamberlain is now Governor of the State of South Carolina beyond any controversy, and remains so until a new Governor shall be duly and legally inaugurated under the Constitution. The Government has been called upon to aid with the military and naval forces of the United States to maintain republican government in the State against resistance too formidable to be overcome by the State authorities. You are directed, therefore, to sustain Governor Chamberlain in his authority against domestic violence until otherwise directed.

U. S. GRANT.

The Secretary of War in transmitting by telegraph this letter to General Ruger, at Columbia, added:

In obeying these instructions you will advise with the Governor, and dispose of your troops in such a manner as may be deemed best in order to carry out the spirit of the above order of the President.

Just at midnight, before the day of the convening of the Legislature, a company of United States soldiers was, upon the request of Governor Chamberlain, marched into the State House and stationed on the second floor in the wide lobby between the Senate Chamber and the Hall of the House of Representatives. As the orders to the soldiers were to keep out of the State House all persons who might unlawfully interfere with the proceedings of the Legislature, sentinels posted at the four entrances to the lower floor of the State House halted and questioned all persons, including even the Supreme Court Judges, who sought to enter the building. Sentinels also stood guard, one on each side, at the entrance to the floor of the House and at the entrance to its gallery. The notorious John B. Dennis, a henchman of Chamberlain, stood at the entrance to the floor of the House to examine the credentials of all who claimed to be members of that body, and to instruct the sentinels whom they should admit.

Meanwhile the Democratic members-elect of the House of Representatives had held two caucuses—one in Carolina Hall[169] in the city of Columbia, three days before, and the other, in the Hall of the House of Representatives, on the day before the Legislature was to convene—to decide upon the course to pursue should the Edgefield and Laurens delegations be denied admission to the House. At the second caucus General Hampton, General John B. Gordon, who had recently been elected United States Senator from Georgia, and General M. W. Gary, who had been elected State Senator from Edgefield County, were present.[170]

Shortly before noon, November 28, the time for the convening of the Legislature, the Democratic members-elect of the House proceeded in a body from Carolina Hall to the State House, the Edgefield members leading and the Laurens members coming next, with General Hampton, Colonel Haskell, and other members of the State Executive Committee following the rest of the members. The column, headed by John C. Sheppard, of Edgefield, was allowed to pass through the entrance of the building downstairs. When, however, it reached the door to the floor of the Hall and the Edgefield members presented their certificates from the Supreme Court showing that

[169]Carolina Hall, one of the first buildings erected in Columbia after Sherman passed through, was built by Major James G. Gibbes with bricks salvaged from the ruins of the city. The old courthouse, near the northeast corner of Main and Washington Streets, having been burned, Carolina Hall was used as the courthouse for several years. Court was held upstairs, while the county offices were downstairs.

Carolina Hall is northwest of the present courthouse, in the very heart of the block in which that building is situated. It faces on an alley which ran from Hampton Avenue, at the back of the present Imperial Hotel, through to Law Range on Washington Street. This alley was a thoroughfare in 1876, but is now closed on the end at Law Range. One standing at the back of Bryan's Book Store finds Carolina Hall just in front of him, somewhat to his right. The building had two stories in 1876, but the upper part was destroyed by fire some years ago.

[170]John G. Guignard, The Wallace House (pamphlet), p. 3. Mr. Guignard was a member of the Wallace House from Aiken County.

they had received a majority of the votes cast, they were refused admittance by Dennis. Thereupon a formal protest was read by Sheppard, and since it had been determined that no further effort would be made to enter the Hall if the Edgefield delegation was refused admittance, the Democrats returned to Carolina Hall, where they organized the House by electing as Speaker, General W. H. Wallace, of Union,[171] and as clerk John T. Sloan, Sr., of Richland.[171a]

Meanwhile, the Republican members, assembled in the Hall of the House of Representatives, had organized by electing E. W. M. Mackey, of Charleston, as Speaker.[172]

The hour of noon, November 28, 1876, was the most critical time for South Carolina in all that critical year. Peace trembled in the balance. An immense crowd of outraged Democrats from all parts of the State packed the plaza in front of the State Capitol. It looked as if these fiercely determined men would at any moment storm the building, brush aside the United States soldiers and take forcible possession of the Hall of the House of Representatives. Had they done so the State House would have been red with blood. Chamberlain and General Ruger sat in the Governor's private office in the right wing of the State House, where they could see from the window the surging mass. Upon the request of Chamberlain, General Ruger sent an officer to find Hampton, who was still in the State House, to ask him to quiet the angry crowd outside.[173] Hampton promptly complied. He appeared at the front entrance to the State House. Immediately the tumult ceased. Every Democrat stood in silence to hear what the revered leader might say. Had he said "Let it be war!" there would

[171]William Henry Wallace was born in Laurens County, S. C., in 1827. He was graduated from the South Carolina College in 1849, admitted to the bar in 1859, and elected to the Legislature from Union County in 1860. He attained the rank of Brigadier General in the Confederate army. He again served in the Legislature from Union County, 1872-1877. He was Judge of the Circuit Court 1877-1893.

[171a]Since the House was composed of 124 members, 63 of whom constituted a quorum, the Democrats contended that if they stayed out of the House altogether, the Republicans, with only 59 members, would lack a quorum. The contention of the Republicans, on the other hand, was that a majority of those *elected* constituted a quorum, and that as only a hundred and sixteen members had been elected (exclusive of those from Edgefield and Laurens Counties) their 59 members gave them a quorum.

[172]E. W. M. Mackey, a native white Republican and bitter partisan, was a continual stirrer-up of strife between the races. While a fearless man, he was unscrupulous, and was one of those who had accepted bribes in the big printing steal. He was a nephew of Judge T. J. Mackey, who had gone over to the Democrats upon the nomination of Hampton.

[173]Wells, p. 157.

have been war; but in a clear, calm voice he pleaded with his followers for peace:

My friends: I am truly doing what I have done earnestly during this whole exciting contest, pouring oil on the troubled waters. It is of the greatest importance to us all, as citizens of South Carolina, that peace should be preserved. I appeal to you all, white men and colored, as Carolinians, to use every effort to keep down violence or turbulence. One act of violence may precipitate bloodshed and desolation. I implore you, then, to preserve the peace. I beg all of my friends to disperse, to leave the grounds of the State House, and I advise all the colored men to do the same. Keep perfectly quiet, leave the streets, and do nothing to provoke a riot. We trust to the law and the Constitution, and we have perfect faith in the justness of our cause.

No sooner had he ended his plea when the crowd, only a few minutes before turbulent and rebellious, dispersed promptly and quietly. In three minutes' time there was scarcely a man to be seen on the State House grounds.

Hampton afterwards modestly spoke of this trying moment: "I was passing through the corridor, when the officer in charge of the troops asked me to help him in quieting a crowd which had assembled in front of the Capitol threatening an attack. There were at least 5,000 men in the crowd. I told them we wanted no disturbance, and asked them to go away. Everyone of them had left within three minutes. Nothing which had yet happened to us was so appalling as that mob, which was friendly to me."[174]

But let two eye-witnesses from outside the State, who were standing near Hampton at the time, tell how he averted probable civil war.

Bradley T. Johnson, who had been a Confederate General, and was then a prominent attorney of Baltimore, wrote Hampton:

"You had only to raise your hand and Ruger's garrison would have been swept off the face of the earth. But you held them [the crowd] back, and I know of no more remarkable illustration of moral force than your control and their obedience —honorable to both. You had only to say, 'There they are— take them!' and the firing on Sumter would have been repeated."[175]

---

[174]Interview with Hampton published in the Boston *Globe*, November 29, 1879, and republished in the Columbia *Register* of December 3, 1879.
[175]Letter published in Columbia *State*, February 7, 1893.

The correspondent of the New York *Herald* wrote his paper under date of November 29, 1876:

"The bearing of South Carolina citizens in the great trial to which they were subjected yesterday was admirable. There has never been a more critical and dangerous conjunction in the history of American politics. The whole country had its attention focused on the proceedings at Columbia and there was a great strain of anxiety and apprehension lest scenes of violence and bloodshed should set the whole country on fire and inaugurate a new civil war. Public passion was in so inflamed a state that a mere spark might have kindled a conflagration of which the consequences would have been appalling. As no spark fell into the dry tinder there we felicitate the country that the period of danger is past.

"The credit of preserving the peace at Columbia yesterday is due to General Wade Hampton, Democratic candidate for Governor. He had only to lift his finger, he had only to signify the slightest assent and the State House would have been rescued from the Federal soldiers and his supporters could have controlled the organization of the Legislature. The Federal troops were only three hundred, and there were at least eight thousand Democrats present in Columbia, accustomed to the use of arms and with arms probably upon their persons, who could have crumpled and annihilated the small Federal force had they given way to their indignation and to their sense of wrong. It is fortunate that they have a leader so strong, so sagacious, so self-possessed and so thoroughly trusted as Wade Hampton. He perfectly understands the situation, and as we may judge by his conduct yesterday, he will make no mistake. . . . His supporters have so much confidence in him that they will do nothing against his wishes and he understands the situation too well to permit any resort to violence."[176]

---

[176]Republished in the Charleston *News and Courier,* December 2, 1876.

CHAPTER XXI

THE DUAL HOUSES

The "rump parliament" of South Carolina, the Mackey House, not so sure of its claim that a majority of the *elected* members constitute a quorum, proceeded immediately to manufacture a quorum which the Republicans could claim was a legal quorum of the total membership of the House. The Democratic members elected from Abbeville, Aiken and Barnwell were, by a resolution, unseated and their places given to Republicans who had been candidates against them, and who had come forward with claims to having been elected. During the proceedings attending the swearing in of the contestants occurred an incident illustrative of the low plane of the Mackey House. A negro, impersonating Silas Cave, a claimant to a seat from Barnwell, was solemnly sworn in. A day or two later Cave showed up and he, in turn, was sworn in with equal solemnity, the other members taking the incident as a matter of course—as nothing out of the ordinary in their varied experience in Reconstruction Legislatures.

The Senate met in its Chamber also at noon.[177] Here the Republicans increased their majority by refusing seats to Gary of Edgefield, Todd of Laurens, and Maxwell of Abbeville, who the returns showed had been elected by large majorities. The Senate now consisted of only thirty members—eighteen Republicans and twelve Democrats. Notice was formally sent to the "House" (meaning thereby the Mackey outfit) that the Senate was organized and ready for business. Against this proceeding the Democratic Senators made strenuous objection and put their objection on record by spreading upon the journal a formal protest against "any recognition of said body pretending to be the House of Representatives in South Carolina."

Meanwhile the Wallace House had gained accessions at the expense of its rival. A few hours after the Wallace House had organized a white Republican of the Mackey House, W. H. Reedish, of Orangeburg, and a negro, J. W. Westberry, of

---

[177]Josephus Woodruff, the shameless bribe-giver, was re-elected Clerk of the Senate.

Sumter, withdrew from the "rump parliament" and joined the
Wallace House.   Two days later, three other members of the
Mackey House, J. S. Bridges, of Newberry, and N. B. Myers
and Tom Hamilton, of Beaufort, all negroes, were persuaded to
change over.   Without the votes of the Edgefield and Laurens
delegations, the Wallace House now had a quorum of the House
of Representatives, for it carried on its roll a majority of
members who had been recognized by the State Board of Canvassers, and who held certificates from the Secretary of State.
The Wallace House held another session, in Carolina Hall, on
the day following its organization, and transacted such business
as came before it.

On the morning of the next day, Thursday, November 30,
the Wallace House, including the delegations from Edgefield
and Laurens, again appeared at the State House to occupy the
Hall of the House of Representatives.   They purposed, of
course, to continue their organization and transact there the
business of the House, without recognizing in any way the
Mackey House organization.   They hoped to do so without
any breach of the peace, and were relying upon the understanding that General Ruger would remove no one from the floor of
the House, nor interfere in any way with the proceedings, unless such action was deemed necessary to preserve order.

Not desiring to attract attention by appearing in the streets
in a body, the members of the Wallace House went in
groups to the eastern entrance to the State House, near the
Supreme Court room, where an officer of the United States
army inspected their credentials, and passed them in.   Once inside the building they moved on, with Colonel Haskell leading
and accompanied by James L. Orr,[178] towards the Hall of the
House.   As they had anticipated by an hour the time for the
assembling of the Mackey House the Democrats found at the
entrance leading to the floor of the Hall, no military guard—
only a sergeant-at-arms and a doorkeeper, both of whom were
negroes, and a deputy United States marshal.   When the
sergeant-at-arms reached out his hand to take the first certificates offered him, Haskell and Orr threw wide open the
doors to the Hall.   Orr, who was of towering form and great
strength, twisted the sergeant-at-arms by the neck, and others,

---

[178]Son of the distinguished Governor of that name.

making braces of their bodies, held the doors open, while the rest rushed into the hall. Speaker Wallace occupied the speaker's stand and all the members found seats.

Soon Speaker E. W. M. Mackey, of the Radical House, walked up the right aisle and approached Speaker Wallace, who was seated in the Speaker's chair. Mackey ascended the rostrum and demanded that Wallace surrender the chair to him. Wallace refused to comply, stating that he was the presiding officer of the lawful House. Then followed the colloquy:

Mackey: "I claim that I was elected Speaker of this House by a legal quorum of members legally sworn in. We do not recognize that any others than those sworn in here on Tuesday last are members of this House, and these men who are visiting this hall without our consent must keep order. I again demand that you, General Wallace, leave this chair."

Speaker Wallace: "I have already declared that I am the lawfully elected Speaker of this House, and must ask you to retire."

Mackey: "The sergeant-at-arms will please step forward and enforce my order."

Speaker Wallace: "The sergeant-at-arms will please step forward and enforce my order."

Two sergeants-at-arms, one from each body, went forward. Democrats and Republicans alike appeared determined to hold their ground, and they crowded around their respective claimants to the speakership. It seemed that bloodshed could not be avoided, so intense was the excitement. Mackey had been given notice that several men had been selected to kill him at once in the event of actual trouble; but, a man of unusual courage, he stood unperturbed upon the rostrum, a ready mark for the first shot that might be fired. Some one handed him a chair and he calmly took a seat beside the Democratic Speaker. He sat beside a man just as brave as himself. General Wallace, whose courage had been proved on many a battlefield, continued to occupy the Speaker's chair with an equal absence of fear.

The tension was relieved when a Democrat made a motion that a committee of six be appointed to seek an adjustment of the situation. Although only the Democrats voted when

Speaker Wallace put the question, for Mackey immediately directed his followers to pay no attention to Wallace nor to any other proceedings arising for the Democratic side, yet the mere fact of there being a motion, and the diversion which was created by voting upon it served to distract both sides from their hostile attitudes.

With its acute phase passed, the situation turned into a test of lungs and endurance between the rival bodies—a contest as to which side could outdo the other in going through the form of legislating. It was a unique sight—two bodies performing in the same hall, and at the same time, the duties, or pretended duties, of the House of Representatives without recognition from either side of the presence of the other. The Wallace House occupied the left of the Hall and the Mackey House the right. All of the Mackey House, except five or six, were negroes. Two Speakers and two clerks sat on the rostrum. Simultaneously, but separately, resolutions and motions were offered and debated by each side. Sometimes two brilliant orations would be going on at the same time. But the most novel proceeding of all was the simultaneous calling of the rolls of the two Houses—the two clerks at the desk reading, in their loudest voices, the names on their respective rolls, and the members on each side answering when their names were called. If either Speaker had to leave the rostrum he would put in his place a member of his party. In this way it was often the case that a white man and a negro would be presiding side-by-side.

Since the members of each House wished to keep their places so as to be ready for anything that might turn up, they stayed in the Hall at nights. As darkness approached the legislative activities would slacken. The tired "law-makers" would lounge about, or seek rest on the floor. The whites were abundantly supplied with meals by the people of Columbia, and they would often generously share them with the negroes, against most of whom they had really no ill feeling, looking upon them as ignorant, and misguided by wicked leaders. The negroes, in turn—for most negroes are born songsters—would enliven the early part of the nights with the loud singing of such songs as "Hold the Fort for Hayes and Wheeler." Every morning each House was again called to order, the roll called, a quorum announced, and legislation similar to that of the day before was carried on.[179]

The two Houses continued to occupy the Hall of the House of Representatives for five days and four nights. On the first day of the dual occupancy of the Hall (Thursday, November 30) General Ruger notified Speaker Wallace that he would be forced to eject the Edgefield and Laurens delegations from the floor of the Hall if they were there on the following day. This retraction of the understanding that he had given the Democrats brought General Ruger a stinging rebuke in the form of a letter signed by Hampton, Gordon and Haskell. "It is proper to say," the letter read, "that we relied upon your honor as a man and your character as a soldier to maintain your pledged position of non-intervention." "Let the American people." the letter added, "behold the spectacle of a brigadier general of the army, seated by the side of Governor Chamberlain in a room in the State House, issuing his orders to a legislative body peacefully assembled in one of the original thirteen commonwealths of the Union."

General Ruger never took the threatened action. However, on Sunday, December 3, information reached Democratic headquarters in Columbia to the effect that a hundred members of the "Hunkey-Dory Club,"[180] of Charleston, composed of negro stevedores, wharf rats and thugs, which had been organized by the Republican leaders in that city to "intimidate and insult the white people, and to embolden and solidify the blacks," were coming to Columbia to eject the Edgefield and Laurens members from the House.[181] The details of the plot as given were that the members of the Hunkey-Dory Club would be smuggled into the committee rooms at night. The next day the Republican members would withdraw from the House, one by one, and when all of them had left, the doors would be opened and "the terriers let in on the rats."

The news was flashed over the wires, and by Monday night

---

[179]Much the greater part of the account in the text of the forcible entrance of the Wallace House into the Hall of the House of Representatives, and of the simultaneous occupation of the Hall by the two Houses, is taken almost verbatim from J. G. Guignard's The Wallace House (pamphlet). Mr. Guignard, as a member of the Wallace House from Aiken, was a participant in the thrilling adventure.

[180]Webster defines "hunkey-dory" as meaning all right—in good condition.

[181]The Hunkey-Dorey Cub, whose members were usually armed with heavy bludgeons, had incited the trouble which led to the Charleston riots, and had long been a menace to that city.—Reynolds, p. 418.

about five thousand men had reached Columbia. Many were Confederate veterans and all came armed, some with Winchesters, some with pistols and others with both. They were grim and determined men who had come for business, and their business was not only to protect the Democratic Legislature, but to take possession of the State House.

Meanwhile all necesary precautions had been taken in the House to resist any effort that might be made to eject the Edgefield and Laurens members. A Democrat of proved courage and coolness was designated to take charge on the floor, and arrangements were made to shoot Mackey to death at the first show of violence which occurred. It was regarded as certain that the killing of Chamberlain would have quickly followed.

The party leaders, however, believed that the preservation of peace was still the only sure way to securing possession of the government, and they advised the avoidance of a conflict with the Hunkey-Dory Club. Consequently, on the morning of Monday, December 4, after the reading of the journal, Speaker Wallace addressed the Democratic House, saying: "With a view of preventing a collision upon this floor in which lives may be lost and blood shed; with a view of submitting to proper and legal arbitrament of all the rights we claim on this floor, the chair is of the opinion that this House should withdraw from this hall." Immediately and quietly the Wallace House left the State House, and returned to its old quarters at Carolina Hall, where it resumed the interrupted session of the legislative day.

However, the many thousands that had come to Columbia were not so easily handled. That night they collected in front of Democratic headquarters, ready and eager to storm the State House. They called for Hampton to lead them. It was almost as critical a moment as when, a few days before, another crowd had surged in front of the State House. Hampton had then quieted the tumult, and now it was his part again to control a multitude. He tactfully addressed the crowd:

"I am glad to see you all here, come to see the State Fair.[182] There is very good stock out there and I hope you will all go to see it, and be very particular to behave in an orderly and quiet manner. I want you

[182]The State Fair, annually held in Columbia, was then in progress.

all to remember that I have been elected Governor of South Carolina, and by the God above I intend to be Governor. Go home and rely on that. I'll send for you whenever I need you."

When Hampton had closed his speech, the crowd, as it had done a few days before, melted from the streets.[183]

The Democrats had carried the legislative tangle to the State Supreme Court (Republican) in order that the Court might decide the question whether the Wallace House or the Mackey House was the lawful House of Representatives, and they won the suit. Two days after the Wallace House had withdrawn from the State House the Supreme Court rendered a decision that "William H. Wallace is the legal speaker of the lawfully-constituted House of Representatives of the State of South Carolina."

The decision gave much encouragement to the white people of the State, yet it had no effect in putting an end to their troubles. A committee, appointed by the Wallace House, appeared before General Ruger to ascertain, now that the highest tribunal in the State had declared it the lawful House, what his attitude would be should the Democratic House again attempt to resume its lawful place in the State House. General Ruger made it known to the committee that, since his orders were that he should give military support to the Chamberlain government, he would, despite the decision of the State Supreme Court, continue to do so. His formal reply read in part: "I would say that if your body should appear at the State House for the purpose of entering the hall of the House

---

[183]From letter of General Bradley T. Johnson to General Hampton, published in the Columbia *State*, February 7, 1893:

"I remember how the wires were hot . . . and how by 9 a. m. we had 2,500 of the old soldier .. the Army of Northern Virginia on the spot and by sundown there were 5,000 of them—and then they were all brought up before the headquarters. . . . That speech, and the yell that responded to it made you Governor. . . . Let South Carolina and South Carolinians remember until the last syllable of recorded time that manliness and courage bore her through the ordeal of 1876, ten thousand times more trying than Cornwallis' or Tarleton's raids or Sherman's dragonade."

From article of Prof. R. Means Davis in the Columbia *State*, April 12, 1902:

"The people, fearing that all hope of a peaceful settlement was ended, were ready to scale the walls of the State House and throw the whole Republican assemblage out of the windows, or even to kill them and destroy the Federal garrison. It was one of those occasions on which men in hot blood commit an act that they will rue bitterly ever after. The task of extermination would not have been difficult. In that gathering were several thousands of the best soldiers the world has ever seen, trained on a hundred battlefields to despise odds, and possessing odds of ten to one, they would have considered the task easy."

of Representatives and should be refused admission by those having charge of the doors, and such persons should apply to the officer in command of the troops at the State House for assistance necessary to prevent you from entering, the present orders to the officer would require him to render such assistance."

Courtesy of *Leslie-Judge Co., Columbia State and W. P. Houseal*

INAUGURATION OF WADE HAMPTON, DECEMBER 14, 1876
FROM PENCIL SKETCH PUBLISHED IN FRANK LESLIE'S WEEKLY, JANUARY, 1877
(Carolina Hall faces west. The top of Richland County Courthouse is seen at its right)

CHAPTER XXII

THE DUAL GOVERNORS

On the day following the withdrawal of the Wallace House from the State House (December 5) the bogus House of Representatives, joined by the Republican Senators, went through the form of canvassing the vote for Governor and Lieutenant Governor. After throwing out the returns from Edgefield and Laurens Counties, the result was announced as follows: Chamberlain, 86,216; Hampton, 83,071; Gleaves, 86,320; Simpson, 82,231. Two days later, Chamberlain went through the form of an inauguration, and the Republican claimants to the other State offices took the oath of office.

Chamberlain's inaugural address was, in the main, a bitter denunciation of the Democrats. He said in part:

If we yield now we shall witness the consummation of a deliberate and cruel conspiracy on the part of the Democratic party of this State to overcome by brute force the political will of a majority of 30,000 of the lawful voters of this State. . . .

I denounce the conduct of the recent election on the part of our political opponents in this State as a vast brutal outrage. Fraud, proscription, intimidation in all forms, violence—ranging through all its degrees up to wanton murder—were its effective methods. . . . It is for us, in the face of open enemies, to show that we understand the cause in which we are engaged, and that no earthly sacrifice is too great to secure the triumph. . . .

There is one thing no man in South Carolina can do, however powerful or desperate he may be, and that is to cause me to abate my hatred or cease my most vigorous resistance of this attempted overthrow and enslavement of a majority of the people of South Carolina. "Here I stand; I can do no otherwise: God be my helper."

Throughout the State the so-called inauguration of Chamberlain was regarded as an insolent defiance of the Supreme Court and a bold attempt at usurpation.[184] Another crowd collected that night on the streets of Columbia. Again Hampton relieved the excitement by telling the crowd to go home and not worry, for he could assure them that he would yet be Governor. This time he made the promise in the memorable words: "The people have elected me Governor, and by the Eternal God I will be Governor or we shall have a military Governor!"

[184]Reynolds, p. 425.

The pretended inauguration of Chamberlain knocked the props from under the position taken by President Grant in his instructions to General Ruger. It will be remembered that Grant then declared that, since Chamberlain continued to be Governor until his successor had qualified, the United States army should and would support him. With the inauguration of Chamberlain for a second time Grant's position ceased to be tenable for Chamberlain could claim no longer to be a hold-over Governor. There is no evidence, however, that this fact caused the least abatement in Grant's hostility towards the white people of South Carolina.

One week after Chamberlain's pretended inauguration (December 14) the lawful House of Representatives, the Democratic Senators meeting with it, tabulated the returns for Governor and Lieutenant Governor. The returns from Edgefield and Laurens Counties were included in the count, which showed that Hampton had a majority of 1,134, and Simpson a majority of 539.

On the same day Hampton was inaugurated as Governor in front of Carolina Hall. There a stand, erected for the purpose, had been banked with wreaths and flowers and draped with the National and State flags. An immense concourse of men and women had gathered to witness the ceremonies, and the fact that, because Chamberlain, backed up by United States troops, held the State House, Hampton had to be inaugurated elsewhere, did not in the least dampen their joy. Conspicuous in the crowd were the Red Shirts, and as Hampton released the Bible on taking the oath, the event was announced by salvos from the cannon of the "Hampton Saluting Club," the successor to the Columbia Flying Artillery Club, which had been "disbanded" by the proclamation of President Grant. When the hero of the hour advanced to the front of the platform to deliver his inaugural address, mighty shouts went up that echoed and re-echoed through the streets. The salvos and the shouts, heard at the State House, only a few blocks away, must have carried discouragement to Chamberlain and his crew, for they came from a united people that did not need Federal bayonets for the support of their government.

At the conclusion of the ceremonies four stalwart young men

raised Hampton in a chair to their shoulders, and bore him to his hotel, the cheering crowd following.

Hampton's inaugural address was brief.   The spirit of optimism and good will, prevailing throughout, contrasted strongly with the bitter and resentful tone of Chamberlain's inaugural address of the week before.   After recounting the reforms to which their platform had pledged the Democrats—honest government, efficient schools and equality before the law for all citizens of South Carolina, of both races and both parties—Hampton's address continued with this promise of an auspicious future for all the people:

> To the faithful observance of the pledges we stand committed, and I, as the representative of the conservative party hold myself bound by every dictate of honor and of good faith to use every effort to have these pledges redeemed fully and honestly. . . .
>
> We owe much of our late success to these colored voters who were brave enough to rise above the prejudice of race and honest enough to throw off the shackles of party in their determination to save the State. To those, who, misled by their fears, their ignorance, or by evil counseling, turned a deaf ear to our appeals, we should not be vindictive but magnanimous.   Let us show to all of them that the true interests of both races can best be secured by cultivating peace and promoting prosperity among all classes of our fellow citizens. . . .   United and working with resolute will and earnest determination, we may hope soon to see the dawn of a brighter day for our State.   God in His infinite mercy grant that it may come speedily, and may He shower the richest blessings of peace and happiness on our whole people.

Deprived of the use of the State House, the Democrats fitted up executive offices for Hampton in a suite of rooms above a store in Columbia.   There he transacted affairs of State, assisted by General Johnson Hagood, who had been elected Comptroller-General, but who had been refused a certificate of election by the State Board of Canvassers.   A secretary and a clerk performed the clerical duties.

Thus the State had two civil governments, each claiming to be legal, and each with executive and legislative departments functioning to a more or less degree.

Shortly after his inauguration Governor Hampton addressed the following demand to Chamberlain:

State of South Carolina,
Executive Chamber,
Columbia, December 18, 1876.

Sir: As Governor of South Carolina, chosen by the people thereof I have qualified in accordance with the Constitution, and I hereby call upon you as my predecessor in office to deliver up to me the great seal of the State, together with the possession of the State House, the public records and all other matters and things appertaining to said office.

Respectfully, your obedient servant,

WADE HAMPTON, Governor.

D. H. Chamberlain, Esq.

To the demand Chamberlain sent the following reply:

State of South Carolina,
Executive Chamber,
Columbia, S. C., December 18, 1876.

Sir: I have received the communication in which you call upon me to deliver to you the great seal, etc., etc.

I do not recognize in you any right to make the foregoing demand, and I hereby refuse compliance therewith.

I am, sir, your obedient servant,

D. H. CHAMBERLAIN,
Governor of South Carolina.

Wade Hampton, Esq.

Simpson, having taken the oath of office as Lieutenant-Governor at the time Hampton was inaugurated, sent a communication to the Senate announcing that he was ready to assume his duties as presiding officer of the Senate; but that body, under control of the Republicans, did not deign to make reply. The Democratic Senators protested without avail against Gleaves' continuing to preside over the Senate.

Both Legislatures elected United States Senators to succeed Thomas J. Robertson, whose term was about to expire, the Democrats of the State Senate acting for this purpose with the lawful House, and the Republican Senators with the bogus House. The Democrats elected General M. C. Butler and the Republicans D. T. Corbin.[185]

Both Legislatures, on December 22, adjourned *sine die*. Among the "laws" passed by the bogus Legislature was one designed for the prosecution of Hampton and others prominent in his government on the charge of "treason." Whatever was at the bottom of this piece of "legislation"—whether it

---

[185]Corbin was a lawyer of some ability, a carpetbagger from Vermont. On first coming to South Carolina he was connected with the Freedmen's Bureau. Later, as District Attorney, he brought upon himself the hatred of the whites by his activity in hunting down and arresting, on flimsy testimony, persons accused of violation of the Ku Klux and other "Force Bills," and by his unjust and vindictive methods in prosecuting such of them as were brought to trial.

was intended for intimidation, or whether it was merely gasconade—it of course gave the Democrats no concern.[186]

Still carrying the responsibility of holding within bounds the impatience of a people fretting over the seeming tardiness of their getting control of the State government, which they had won after a long and arduous struggle, there devolved upon Hampton, with the adjournment of the Legislature, the further task of keeping "the Ship of State afloat."

One of the first matters to receive Hampton's attention after becoming Governor was that of the county governments which had become considerably disarranged, owing to the unsettled condition of the State government. Where there was a vacancy in the office of trial justice (magistrate) or other county office, or where the incumbent was guilty of corruption, or other malfeasance, Hampton appointed to the position a reputable citizen. The county officials who held on to their offices acknowledged, one by one, the authority of the Hampton government, and the Circuit Judges also recognized its authority.

As the Republicans had control of the State Senate, that body had continued to act with the Mackey House. Consequently, the Democratic House, realizing that it had no legal right to do so alone, refrained from levying taxes and, therefore, from making appropriations to meet the expenses of its State government. The Democrats had, however, taken legal steps to prevent the banks then holding State funds from paying out any part of them to the Chamberlain government, but this action proved unnecessary, for the banks were quite willing to co-operate with the Hampton government by honoring its drafts instead of those of the Chamberlain government.[187]

But, as these funds were not sufficient to run the government, the Democratic Legislature had provided another way for raising money. Since it could not legally levy taxes, the Leg-

[186]Wells, p. 171.

"An amusing effort of the Mackey body was seen in the passage of 'a bill to prevent and punish any person or persons for setting up, or attempting to set up, or maintaining a government of the State in opposition to the legitimate and lawful government.' Offenders against this proposed law were punishable with a fine of not less than $20,000 or more than $100,000, and imprisonment for a term not less than ten or more than forty years. To enforce this measure the Governor was to be authorized to use the militia and the constabulary, and to call on the President for troops. The pretended passage of this measure afforded some amusement to the supporters of the lawful State government."—Reynolds, p. 434.

[187]Wells, p. 174.

islature passed a resolution authorizing Governor Hampton
to request all taxpayers to advance amounts equal to one-fourth
of the taxes they had paid the previous year with the understanding that the amounts so advanced would be deducted
from the taxes to be paid when the Democrats should be in
complete control. Acting under this resolution, Hampton
called for contributions, but limited the call to ten per cent. of
the amount that the resolution authorized him to ask for.
The response was immediate. At mass meetings held all over
the State taxpayers pledged themselves not to pay a cent of
taxes to the Chamberlain government, and to make immediately the advances requested by the Hampton government.
Chamberlain was condemned in unmeasured terms at most of
the mass meetings. At a very large meeting in Charleston he
was denounced "as a usurper and a traitor to the State and
her laws."[188] In an amazingly short time the "receivers" or
"special agents" appointed by Hampton to receive the contributions from their respective counties, reported them so very
large that Hampton found it unnecessary to make a call for
a second installment of the amount authorized in the resolution of the Legislature.[189]

On the other hand the Chamberlain government was steering
a rocky course. The Republican Legislature did not have the
scruples of the Democratic Legislature about the legality of
levying taxes, and, although it had an unlawful House, it
attempted to levy them. But a serious predicament for the
Chamberlain government soon developed. The few taxpayers
who favored the Chamberlain government were chary about
paying taxes levied by a Legislature that the Supreme Court

[188]The rapidity with which the white people's estimate of Chamberlain's character fluctuated, during Reconstruction, is striking. As late as 1874 they classed
him among the carpetbaggers who were looting the State, and approved of the
severe denunciation of him in the State Democratic platform of that year. By
1875 he was in high favor on account of his course as Governor, and especially
for the stand he took at the time of the election of Moses and Whipper to judge-
ships. At the beginning of 1876 a majority of the white people favored supporting him for another term as Governor. By early summer his reputation had
waned considerably, and by the fall of 1876 it had sunk to a point as low as it
had ever been—so low that scarcely a white person in the State had a good word
to say for him. And anticipating somewhat, it may be added, that Chamberlain,
some years after Reconstruction returned to South Carolina, spending considerable
time in the State and was then cordially received by the white people who had
formerly been his most bitter political enemies.

[189]Dr. James Woodrow (uncle of Woodrow Wilson), who was owner of the
Presbyterian Publishing House, in Columbia, offered to do the public printing for
the Hampton government, and wait for his pay until such time as payment could
be made—an offer which was gratefully accepted.

of the State had declared unlawful. To the low condition to which the Republicans had sunk the State's credit was now added, as a deterrent to financiers, the doubt as to the validity of the Chamberlain government; and Chamberlain and his henchmen found that they could not borrow money on the State's name. Great difficulty was met even in securing funds enough to pay the ordinary expenses of government. Carpetbaggers and scalawags, accustomed to fatten upon the State's treasury, began to lose heart as they saw opportunities for "good stealing" vanishing; while the poor negroes, though they had never succeeded in getting very much of the loot, seeing that the prospects for "pickings" were fast disappearing, began to weaken in their loyalty to the "Grand old Party." Discredited, both within the State and without, the Chamberlain government wobbled along in some fashion with the one remaining hope—that the authorities at Washington would yet intervene to abolish the Hampton government.[190]

All the time that the contest for the State government was going on in South Carolina the Presidential election was also in dispute. The electoral votes of several States were claimed by both political parties. Tilden, the Democratic candidate, needed only one contested vote to become President, while Hayes, the Republican candidate, needed them all. Among the States whose electoral votes were in dispute was South Carolina. Soon after the elections representatives from both the Democratic and the Republican national organizations appeared in South Carolina to look after their respective party interests. Their maneuvering for the electoral votes of the State added much to the perplexity of the situation. The year 1876 passed out with a double strain upon the nerves of the people of South Carolina—a contest for control of the State government and a contest for control of the national government.

---

[190]Conditions had become so bad in the asylum and the penitentiary that the Republican officials of those institutions were compelled to appeal to the Hampton government for money with which to keep the inmates from starving.

CHAPTER XXIII

Withdrawal of the Federal Troops—Collapse of the Carpetbag-Negro Government

An account has already been given of the proceedings in the State Supreme Court, instituted by the Democrats, that resulted in a decision by that tribunal that the Wallace House was the lawful House of Representatives. It was now determined to prepare a test case that would cause the State Supreme Court to make a decision as to who was the lawful Governor. In a search of the penitentiary for a prisoner deserving of clemency, a negro woman, Tilda Norris by name, was selected. On February 9, 1877, Hampton granted her a pardon. The superintendent of the penitentiary declining to recognize a pardon issued by Hampton as Governor, refused to release her. Thereupon, Tilda Norris, claiming to have been pardoned by the Governor of the State, brought action in the State Supreme Court to compel the superintendent of the penitentiary to set her free. The Court was composed of three members, F. J. Moses, Sr., Chief Justice, and A. J. Willard and J. J. Wright, Associate Justices.[191] As the Chief Justice was ill at the time, the two Associate Justices composed the Court in the hearing of the case. They concurred in issuing an order upon the superintendent of the penitentiary to release the prisoner from custody. Meantime, however, Justice Wright's political associates, white and black, had brought such pressure upon him to reverse his decision that, before the order was filed in the Court, Wright filed an opinion retracting his reasons for

---

[191]It is worthy of note that the three elements constituting the Republican party in the State—scalawags, carpetbaggers and negroes—each had a representative on the court. Chief Justice Moses was a lawyer of marked ability, who had practiced his profession in Sumter for many years before the war. His renegade son, the "Robber Governor," who bore his full name, has thrown a dark cloud about the name; yet it should not be forgotten that the character of Chief Justice Moses was above that of the average South Carolina Republican of Reconstruction times. The illness which prevented the Chief Justice from serving at this time terminated fatally on March 6, and Judge Willard was later elected by the Democratic Legislature to succeed him as Chief Justice. Willard, who was from New York, was a profound student of the law. He had come to South Carolina in the early days of Reconstruction as lieutenant-colonel of a negro regiment, and had afterwards been an official of the Freedmen's Bureau. Wright, the negro Associate Justice, was a native of Pennsylvania. He was of very limited ability and owed his position on the Supreme Court to the fact that the Republican negroes, wishing one of their race to sit on that tribunal and seeming about to elect Whipper, the Democratic members of the Legislature voted for Wright to spare the State the disgrace of Whipper.

having signed the order and declaring, "I now revoke, recall and cancel said order so far as my signature may have given it sanction." Justice Willard, naturally surprised and indignant at his colleague's indefensable course, filed an opinion, which, after stating the fact of Justice Wright's having signed the order, set forth at length his (Willard's) reasons for signing. The opinion in effect adjudged Hampton to be the legal Governor of South Carolina. The superintendent of the penitentiary thereupon discharged Tilda Norris from the institution.

United States troops remained quartered in the State House. There was no longer, however, any reason for their being there, in the face of the two decisions of the legally constituted State court of highest authority, except Grant's determination to continue to support the Chamberlain government despite these decisions; for there was now no disorder whatever. The Hampton government was functioning each day more effectively. The presence of the United States troops, however, kept the tension severe. Aside from the natural repugnance of a free people to military occupation of their Capitol, the soldiers were the only obstacle preventing complete control of the affairs of the State from passing to her decent citizenry. The Hampton government, therefore, appealed to Congress in a memorial submitted to the United States Senate, showing that its officials were legally elected, and praying that Congress would put a stop to the unwarranted interference of the United States troops in the affairs of the State, and would take such further action as would enable the State officials peacefully to perform the duties of the offices to which they had been elected.

The Chamberlain government was quick to send to Congress a counter-memorial, in which it was claimed that Chamberlain and his associates constituted the lawful State government. The old charge of the lawlessness of the white people—the time-worn cry of fraud and intimidation—was again used to bolster up the plea that United States troops were necessary for the support of the lawful (Chamberlain) government.

The request in the Republican memorial that the United States should continue to protect the Chamberlain government "against domestic violence now threatened by Wade Hampton

and others falsely styling themselves officials of said State"
brought from the Democrats the retort:

"The corridors of the Capitol still resound with the measured
tread of the sentinel, and bristling bayonets proclaim to the
favored few who are permitted without molestation to enter
its portals, in language not to be misunderstood—*inter arma
silent leges*. In defiance of the Constitution and of the will of
the people lawfully expressed at the ballot box the Governor,
Lieutenant-Governor and the House of Representatives are
still excluded from the State House by armed troops of the
Federal government. Mr. Chamberlain and his pretended
government are supported and upheld by them and by them
alone."

As the partisan Republicans controlling the United States
Senate approved of the course pursued by President Grant
towards South Carolina, no action was taken upon the me-
morials, and United States troops continued to guard Chamberlain in the State House.

Grant was soon to go out of the President's office, but he
sent a parting fling at South Carolina. The rifle clubs, it will
be remembered, had been disbanded by proclamation of President Grant. After the inauguration of Hampton the members of these clubs had. organized themselves into military
companies which had been accepted by the Hampton government as part of the State militia. Arrangements had been made
for some of the companies to parade in Charleston and Columbia on February 22, in commemoration of Washington's
birthday. By Grant's direction, Lieutenant-Colonel Black
of the United States army, stationed in Columbia, sent a communication to Governor Hampton's office to the effect:
"His Excellency, the President of the United States, directs me
to notify you that the members of the so-called rifle clubs, who
under his proclamation of 17th October last were instructed to
disband, are not to make any public demonstration, or parade,
on 22nd instant, as it is said to be contemplated. . . . My
orders require me to see that no such parade takes place."

Governor Hampton, thereupon, issued a proclamation calling
upon the military companies to postpone the parade. He took
the opportunity afforded by the proclamation to administer to
Grant a rebuke that is a classic:

I hereby call upon these organizations to postpone to some future day this manifestation of their respect to the memory of that illustrious President whose highest ambition it was, as it was his chief glory, to observe the Constitution and to obey the laws of the country.

If the arbitrary commands of a Chief Executive who has not sought to emulate the virtues of Washington deprive the citizens of this State of the privilege of joining publicly in paying reverence to that day so sacred to every American patriot we can at least show by our obedience to constituted authority, however arbitrarily exercised, that we are not unworthy to be the countrymen of Washington.

We must, therefore, remit to some more auspicious period, which I trust is not far distant, the exercise of our right to commemorate the civic virtues of that unsullied character who wielded his sword only to found and perpetuate that American constitutional liberty which is now denied to the citizens of South Carolina.

It is hardly conceivable that the rebuke made an impression upon a President who had uniformly sided against the better class of white people in South Carolina in favor of the leaders of his own party in the State, most of whom very soon thereafter stood stripped before the people of the country as self-confessed criminals.

The white people could only hope for relief when the new President should take office. But the question as to who the new President would be, was not settled until March 3, the day before he should assume the duties. All the contested electoral votes having been finally awarded to Hayes, however, he was declared to have been elected.

While the Presidency was still unsettled, Governor Hampton had addressed identical letters to Tilden and Hayes, in order that the one who should become President would have a correct statement regarding the status of affairs in South Carolina, and would have the assurance from him that the Hampton government condemned and would continue to condemn any solution of the existing political problem except through lawful and peaceful channels.

The mere fact that Hampton had sent a letter to Hayes, and had sent it by Judge T. J. Mackey, a South Carolina Republican, who had supported Hampton, yet favored Hayes, gave rise to a rumor that a bargain had been made whereby Hampton and his associates would make the election returns of South Carolina give Hayes a majority of the votes cast in the State and Hayes would, upon becoming President, remove the United States troops from South Carolina. The rumor was widely published in newspapers and caused considerable stir throughout the country. Color seemed to be lent to the rumor by the fact that while the Democrats of South Carolina, during the progress of the campaign, were loyal to the national party, and solicitous for its success, all other considerations with them were necessarily more or less subordinated to the life and death struggle which they were making for home rule, and by the fact that the returns, as finally tabulated, gave a majority of the votes of the State to Hampton and to Hayes.[192] At the time that the charge originated Hampton denied, both for himself and his associates, that such a bargain had been made through Judge Mackey or anyone else. The State Democratic Executive Committee also made denial. The charge was so baseless, and the characters of Hampton and his associates in the campaign of 1876 are so high that the matter would not be worthy of mention or of refutation but for the fact that the charge still lingers in the minds of uninformed persons, especially outside the State.

As a matter of fact two prominent lawyers from a distance, Judges Denny and Settle, who were in the State representing the interests of the National Republican party, made such a proposition, but Hampton indignantly spurned it.[193]

President Hayes, whose views on government were naturally averse to the rule of force, said in his inaugural address:

Let me assure my countrymen of the Southern States that it is my earnest desire to regard and promote their truest interests—the interests

[192]It is not an unusual occurrence in the history of American politics for the vote of a State to go to the national ticket of one party and the State ticket of the other. State or local issues often enter to make possible this result. One does not have far to seek for the reasons for it in the election of 1876 in South Carolina. The whites in their proselyting impressed upon the negro "Vote for Hampton!" "Vote for Hampton!" and negroes, thinking they had, in voting for Hampton, done enough for their white friends, also voted for Hayes. The white Republicans of the State who supported Hampton did not forswear their allegiance to the Republican party, and they, too, voted for Hayes. The majorities in the State for both Hayes and Hampton were very small and are easily accounted for by the negroes and whites who voted for Hayes and Hampton.

[193]In a letter to Governor Hampton, published in the Columbia State, February 7, 1893, General Bradley T. Johnson writes:

"Judges Denny and Settle, who represented the Republican National Committee at Columbia, proposed to you in the presence of Gordon and myself, that if you would say to the crowd that came to your headquarters every night that you believed that Hayes had carried the State, then the State government should be turned over to you. You promptly replied that Gordon and Johnson would go over the returns with an expert, Denny and Settle being present, and that you would announce the result as certified by all of us. To this Settle replied, laughing: 'Oh, we have had our game with that pack, and have thrown them away.' You then said, 'I will not make such a declaration to be President of the United States.'"

See also letter of General John B. Gordon, published in the Columbia State, February 7, 1893, and the letter of Colonel A. C. Haskell, chairman of the State Democratic Executive Committee, January 22, 1877, published in the newspapers of the time.

of the white and colored people both equally—and to put forth my best effort in behalf of a civil policy which will forever wipe out in our public affairs the color line and the distinction between North and South, to the end that we may have not merely a united North or a united South, but a united country.

These kind words, the first the South had had from the Chief Executive of the nation in many a long year, were tidings of hope to the Southern people, especially in South Carolina and Louisiana, the only states that had not yet succeeded in ridding themselves of the carpetbag-negro governments.[194] The broad patriotism of the inaugural address also elicited hearty response in the North. The right-thinking people of that section, disgusted by the continued gross corruption of the carpetbag-negro governments, and wearied with the stories, year after year, of fraud, violence and bloodshed in the South, had awakened to the realization that the power of the United States government was, for partisan purposes, being used to perpetuate a blot upon civilization.

In fulfilment of the policy announced in his inaugural address, President Hayes promptly took up for consideration the conditions in South Carolina with a view to securing for the State "a peaceful and orderly organization of a single and undisputed State government" and to put "an end as speedily as possible to all appearance of intervention of the military authority of the United States in the political derangements which affect the government and afflict the people of South Carolina."[195] He requested both Hampton and Chamberlain to go to Washington to present to him in person their views as to how this much-to-be-desired result could best be accomplished. In response to the request Hampton and Chamberlain went immediately to Washington.

It should be borne in mind that the people of South Carolina never asked for recognition of their State government by the United States government. The people themselves had chosen their government and it needed no recognition from another source. All they asked of the United States government was that it put an end to the use of its military authority for the

---

[194]The situation in Louisiana was similar to the situation in South Carolina. Both parties claimed to have carried the State in the election of 1876, and, in consequence, there were dual governments, with United States troops supporting the carpetbag-negro government. President Hayes removed the troops from Louisiana on April 20, 1877, and control of the State then passed to the white people.
[195]The words quoted are contained in the letters of President Hayes to Hampton and Chamberlain, which were identical in context.

purpose of interfering with the lawful State government in the peaceful performance of its duties. Governor Hampton made this matter clear in a speech to the people of Columbia on the eve of his departure for Washington:

> I go to Washington simply to state before the President the fact that the people of South Carolina have elected me Governor of that State. I go there to say to him that we ask no recognition from any President. We claim the recognition from the votes of the people of the State. I go there to assure him that we are not fighting for party, but that we are fighting for the good of the whole country. I am going there to demand our rights—nothing more—and, so help me God, to take nothing less.

Hampton, in his interview with the President, told him that all he asked for was the withdrawal of the troops, and he pledged himself that, in the event of their removal, no acts of violence would occur and that the rights of all citizens would be respected. Chamberlain asserted positively to the President that he would not be able to maintain his position without the aid of troops. At a cabinet meeting, following close upon the interviews, it was unanimously decided, after a full discussion, to remove the troops from the State House on April 10.

Hampton's journey to and from Washington was a continual ovation. At every place, even in other States, where his train stopped, people flocked to the station to give him enthusiastic greeting.

The news of the successful termination of Hampton's mission to Washington, sent over the wires ahead of his return, set the people of South Carolina almost wild with joy. In Columbia an immense crowd from every part of the State assembled to welcome the hero's home-coming. The demonstration they made was such as has never been seen, before or since, in South Carolina. Hampton made a brief speech, congratulating the people and promising them that he would restore peace and good government to their distressed State.

Chamberlain issued an address, "To the Republicans of South Carolina," on April 10—the day for the withdrawal of the troops—announcing that it was useless for him to continue the contest, for, while his title to the office of Governor upon every legal or moral ground was clear and perfect, he had been, by the removal of the troops, deprived of the power of enforcing his rights. While forbearing to criticize him, he prayed that future events might justify the decision of the President.

At noon on April 10, the officer in charge of the troops at the State House—a detachment of about thirty men—formed them in the corridor downstairs, and giving the command "two's right," marched them from the building by the south door.

Deprived of the soldiers, the carpetbag-negro government collapsed without a struggle. On April 11, 1877, at 12 o'clock, Chamberlain turned over the Governor's office to Hampton, and the final curtain was rung down upon the most soul-stirring drama which was ever enacted in South Carolina.[196]

Such is the story, in brief, of Reconstruction in South Carolina. It would require volumes to chronicle in detail all the events and phases of Reconstruction in this State alone during the stirring years 1865–1877; yet, all the Southern States suffered that were subjected to the Reconstruction Acts of Congress.

In Virginia, North Carolina and Texas, where the whites were in the majority, and in Georgia, where they were about equal to the negroes in numbers, the Reconstruction governments were soon overthrown, and, as a consequence, these States suffered but little. Florida remained long under carpetbag-negro rule, but on account of its then undeveloped condition, there was not much opportunity in that State for plunder. Alabama, Mississippi, Louisiana and Arkansas, like South Carolina, were sunk deep in degradation by the debauchery of gangs of the basest of white men and a mass of ignorant negroes recently released from slavery; and South Carolina was the greatest sufferer of them all.

In summing up the story of Reconstruction, the first thought that occurs to one is, how utterly futile was the scheme of Reconstruction which Stevens, Morton and others of that ilk sought to fasten upon the South by means of Federal bayonets. The outgrowth of sectional animosity, and nurtured in a school of race antagonism, their scheme was, from its beginning, doomed to inevitable disaster.

---

[196]The Republicans who laid claim to the other State offices surrendered them soon afterwards, so that those who had been lawfully elected to these offices were in full possession of them by May first.

The lesson which the white people of the South learned at such bitter cost, and which they should take to their hearts forever, is that the negro must never again be allowed to gain an ascendency in politics; and that, to prevent such a calamity, the whites must ever stand with a united front, no matter what political differences they may have among themselves.

And, finally, there is the disturbing thought that, though fate has decreed that the two races shall live together in the South, we are no nearer a solution of the problem than was Chamberlain, the New England abolitionist, when he came to South Carolina over half a century ago—a problem that Chamberlain afterwards acknowledged to be "a burden greater than any before put on men of our race." We should remember, however, that the negro was faithful as a slave, and that he is not to blame for Reconstruction, since, in his ignorance, he was then the dupe of wicked and designing white men. As the races have to live in the South, side by side, the white man, because he is of the superior race, owes it to himself that he treat the negro with kindness and consideration. This was the creed of Hampton, the great leader of both races, and he followed it in precept and practice. He said to the negroes just after the War of Secession, and his words are as true now as they were then: "Why should we not be friends? Are you not Southern men, as we are? Is not this your home as well as ours? Does not the glorious Southern sun above us shine alike for both of us? Did not this soil give birth to all of us? And will we not all alike, when our troubles and trials are over, sleep in that same soil on which we first drew breath?"

APPENDIX

Governors of South Carolina, 1868–1886

The collapse of the carpetbag-negro government was the signal for the migration northward of the birds of prey of every hue who had fastened themselves upon the State.

R. K. Scott, the first Republican Governor of the State, returned to his home in Ohio. On Christmas Day, 1880, he shot and killed a young man named Drury, who had been drinking with Scott's young son. Scott was expostulating with Drury when the killing occurred. He was tried and acquitted, his defense being that his pistol was accidentally discharged. Scott died in 1900.

D. H. Chamberlain moved to New York on leaving South Carolina, and engaged in the practice of law. In 1878, he was jointly indicted with other leaders of the Republican party in South Carolina on a charge of conspiracy in connection with certain frauds committed, in 1870, by the Land Commission, of which, as Attorney General, Chamberlain was ex-officio a member. This case was *nol prossed,* however, in 1881.

After leaving the State, Chamberlain turned a complete somersault politically, landing on the Democratic side, and voting for Cleveland for President in 1882. All the preconceived ideas of his youth underwent a radical change, and he retracted all his former utterances in regard to the negro question and the South.

In the early 80's Chamberlain returned to South Carolina as the receiver for the South Carolina Railroad, and spent several years here. Towards the latter part of his life, he suffered from ill health, and spent some time in South Carolina. On both occasions of his return to the State, he was received in a friendly way by the leading people of Columbia. He died in Italy, where he had gone for his health, in 1907, in the seventy-seventh year of his age.

F. J. Moses, Jr., "the Robber Governor," became a victim of the drug habit. On leaving South Carolina, he went North, where he became a professional begger and swindler. On more than one occasion he saw the inside of jails and almshouses on account of theft or vagrancy. He spent a considerable time in New York, where he became notorious. Having a good address, his favorite method of obtaining money there was to pass himself off for some well-known Southerner, and persuade New York business men to cash checks which he had forged, varying in amounts from $100 to $300. On convictions growing out of several of these cases, Moses served a considerable term on Blackwell's Island. One morning, in 1906, when in the sixty-eighth year of his age, he was found dead from asphyxiation in his lodging house in Winthrop, Massachusetts.

Wade Hampton was re-elected Governor in 1878. On November 8 of that year, by what seemed a cruel irony of fate, the gallant warrior, who had passed unscathed through a score of battles, met with an accident while hunting that caused him to lose a leg. For a time following the accident, his life was despaired of, and, on November 20, public prayers were offered for the beloved leader in all the churches of the State. When the Legislature met that year, Hampton was elected United States Senator, and he resigned the office of Governor in February, 1879. He served two terms as Senator. In 1893, President Cleveland appointed him United States Commissioner of Railroads, and he held that position until the change in the National administration in 1897, when he retired to private life.

In the spring of 1899, Hampton's residence on the Camden road was accidentally destroyed by fire. He was then in his eighty-second year, and he had very limited means. Immediately, friends of his, both within and without the State, without Hampton's knowledge, subscribed generously to a fund with which they built the handsome residence, 1800 Senate Street, and presented it to him, over his strenuous protest.

Here Hampton resided until April 11, 1902, when he passed away in his eighty-fifth year—exactly twenty-five years from the day when he had redeemed the State and had entered upon the office of Governor. Although his funeral, because of his dying request, was not a military one, the gathering at the bier was the largest of the kind ever seen in South Carolina—larger even than the gathering at the funeral of John C. Calhoun. People attended from every quarter of the State—the number estimated at twenty thousand—and a considerable proportion of them were negroes. They demonstrated by their sorrow the love and esteem in which the departed hero was held by all classes of people in the State.

Hampton's tomb is in Trinity churchyard, while on the Capitol square, just opposite, stands the handsome equestrian statue to his memory, "erected by the State of South Carolina and her citizens," which was unveiled on November 20, 1906. W. D. Simpson, who was elected Lieutenant-Governor on the Hampton ticket in 1876, succeeded to the office of Governor when Hampton went to the Senate. Simpson was born in Laurens County, in 1823. He graduated from the South Carolina College in 1843, and was admitted to the bar in 1846. As Lieutenant-Governor and ex-officio President of the Senate, Simpson's tact and firmness in dealing with the situation, when he took his seat as the presiding officer of the Senate, in 1877, was a considerable factor in establishing the Democrats firmly in the saddle. He filled the office of Governor until 1880, when he was elected Chief Justice of the Supreme Court of the State, T. B. Jeter, of Union, President pro tem of the Senate, filling out the unexpired term as Governor. Judge Simpson was re-elected Chief Justice in 1886, but died in 1890, before the completion of his second term of six years.

Johnson Hagood, who was Governor from 1880 to 1882, had been one of the most illustrious brigadier generals whom South Carolina furnished the Confederacy. He was born in Barnwell County in 1829, and graduated at the Citadel Academy in 1847. Hagood was the manager of the Hampton campaign in Barnwell County in 1876, and conducted it with signal success. He was elected Comptroller General in that year. At the expiration of his term as Governor, in 1882, he was not a candidate for re-election, and he retired to private life.

Governor Hagood was chairman of the Board of Visitors of the Citadel Academy from 1878 to 1892. It was largely due to his efforts that the Academy, which had been closed since the War of Secession, was re-opened in 1883, and much of the success of the institution in later years has come from the foundation then laid for it by Hagood. He died in 1898.

Hugh S. Thompson, who was elected Governor in 1882, was born in Charleston in 1836, although his parents were residents of Greenville County. He graduated at the Citadel Academy in 1856. A school teacher by profession, Thompson had made a reputation as principal of the Columbia Male Academy prior to 1876, when he was elected State Superintendent of Education. He was re-elected to that office in 1878, and again in 1880. As State Superintendent of Education, Thompson evolved with such success order out of the chaos in which Reconstruction had left the schools that he is regarded as the founder of the public-school system of the State.[196a] On account of his work for the schools he was promoted to Governor in 1882. He was re-elected in 1884.

Near the close of Thompson's second term as Governor, in 1886, he resigned to accept the position of Assistant Secretary of the Treasury under President Cleveland, the Lieutenant Governor, John C. Sheppard, becoming Governor for the rest of the term. When Cleveland was defeated for re-election, in 1888, his Republican successor, President Harrison, appointed Thompson the Democratic member of the United States Civil Service Commission, which office he filled until 1892. In that year he resigned to accept the position of Comptroller of the New York Life Insurance Company, which required his removal to New York. He filled this position until the time of his death, which occurred in 1904.[197]

[196a]"The real beginning of the State school system of South Carolina dates from about 1877, after the close of the Reconstruction period," Macmillan's Cyclopedia of Education, p. 370.

[197]The following appeared in the *New York Times* of December 4, 1904: A few years ago, ex-Governor Hugh S. Thompson, of South Carolina, was asked by the Gridiron Club [of Washington] to make an address at one of the famous banquets. Shortly before the time for his speech arrived, the head-waiter [a negro] approached him, saying, "Governor, is there anything I can get for you?"
"A small cigar," answered the distinguished speaker.
Proffering a box and receiving a coin for the service, the waiter said: "Governor, do you remember me?"
"No," replied Governor Thompson, looking at the negro keenly.
"Like yourself," said the waiter, simply, "I am an ex-Governor of South Carolina."
And then Governor Thompson recalled Richard H. Gleaves, one-time acting Governor of South Carolina.
(NOTE: In 1875, when Chamberlain was temporarily absent from the State, Gleaves had acted as Governor for a few days.)

Chamberlain's Political Transformation

The following excerpts from Chamberlain's article in the *Atlantic Monthly* for April, 1901, and from a pamphlet which he wrote in 1904, entitled, "Present Phases of Our So-Called Negro Problem," will afford some idea of the remarkable transformation which occurred in his political views after he left South Carolina.

* * * *

"I find myself forced by my experience and observation to say that perhaps our first practical aim should be to undo, as far as possible, what we have heretofore done for the negro since his emancipation, namely, the inspiring in him the hope or dream of sharing with the white race [in this country] a social or political equality; for whoever will lay aside wishes and fancies and look at realities, will see that these things are impossibilities within any measurable range of time if ever."

* * * *

"A tremendous effort has been made here [in this country] to establish political equality between the two races—an effort which resulted directly in shocking and unbearable misgovernment wherever the negro race predominated. This, in turn, inevitably aroused the fierce antagonism and hate of the white race. In the desperate struggle of the white race to throw off its political bondage to the negro, violence and fraud, in their many forms, resulted. The triumph of the white race in this struggle left the relations of the two races embittered to a high degree. Generations will be needed to overcome completely the exacerbations and animosities which are the direct fruit of the attempt to establish by force of law a political equality between the two races."

* * * *

"If the canvass of 1876 had resulted in the success of the Republican party, that party could not, for want of materials, even when aided by the Democratic minority, have given pure, or competent administration. The vast preponderance of ignorance and incapacity in that party, aside from downright dishonesty, made it impossible."

"I do not know of one . . . white man, of good character and of responsible standing, who has lived in the South five years since 1876, and been identified with the interests of both races, who has not become . . . a hearty supporter of the mass of the Southern whites in their relation to the negro . . . a supporter of the resolve of the whites to keep the negro out of all practical control or influence in political or public matters, as far as it can be done within the law, and, above all, wholly separate and apart from the whites in all social relations."

* * * *

"The North generally, and the people the world over, are making the great mistake of thinking that education, meaning book knowledge, or literary or academic training, is the great cure for all of the negro's faults and failings. No greater mistake could be made. The three R's are all the average negro needs. After that, industrial training, the training of the hand and eye for work, is all that will help him. More than this is positively harmful."

* * * *

"Man for man, I do not see how we, of the North, or particularly of New England, are better than the people of South Carolina or Alabama. They [Southerners] have, in fact, one great quality which, I think, puts them above most of us—I mean the high, almost highest, great quality—fortitude . . . of this, the Southern people have given the last full proof. . . . They have their faults, no doubt; but, for my part, I am proud of them for countrymen, and I am ready to trust them with any problem they may meet. Once I did not think as I think now; make the most of that, as you are sure to do. But do you imagine that I am going to continue to live in 'a fool's paradise' after I have found it out?"

* * * *

"I adopt and echo the reported last great message of the dying soldier and statesman, Wade Hampton: 'God bless all my people, white and black!'"

DEMOCRATIC MEMBERS OF LEGISLATURE, 1876

SENATORS

Abbeville, J. C. Maxwell
Aiken, A. P. Butler
Barnwell, J. M. Williams
Chesterfield, W. Augustus Evans
Edgefield, M. W. Gary
Greenville, S. C. Crittenden
Horry, William L. Buck

Laurens, R. P. Todd
Lexington, H. A. Meetze
Marion, R. G. Howard
Oconee, J. W. Livingston
Pickens, R. E. Bowen
Spartanburg, Gabriel Cannon
Union, Thomas B. Jeter

York, I. D. Witherspoon

Total 15

THE WALLACE HOUSE

Abbeville—W. K. Bradley, R. R. Hemphill, F. A. Connor, William Hood, J. L. Moore.
Aiken—C. E. Sawyer,* J. J. Woodward, L. M. Asbill, J. G. Guignard.
Anderson—H. R. Vandiver, R. W. Simpson, W. C. Brown, James L. Orr.
Barnwell—I. S. Bamberg, John W. Holmes, L. W. Youmans, W. A. Rountree, Robert Aldrich.
Chesterfield—J. C. Coit, D. T. Redfearn.
Colleton—H. E. Bissell, J. M. Cummins, S. E. Parler, William Maree (negro), R. Jones.
Edgefield—W. S. Allen, J. C. Sheppard,† James Callison, T. E. Jennings, H. A. Shaw.
Greenville—J. W. Gray, J. F. Donald, J. T. Austin, J. S. Westmoreland.
Horry—L. D. Bryan, J. K. Cooper.
Laurens—J. B. Humbert, J. W. Watts, W. D. Anderson.
Lancaster—J. B. Ervin, J. C. Blakeney.
Lexington—G. Leaphart, G. Muller.
Marion—J. G. Blue, J. McRae, R. H. Rogers, J. P. Davis.
Marlboro—Philip M. Hamer, Thomas N. Edens.
Oconee—B. F. Sloan, J. S. Verner.
Pickens—D. F. Bradley, E. S. Bates.
Spartanburg—W. P. Compton, J. W. Wofford, E. S. Allen, Charles Petty.
Union—W. H. Wallace, G. D. Peake, William Jefferies.
York—A. E. Hutchison, J. A. Deal, W. E. Byers, B. H. Massey.

Total 64.

---

*Claude E. Sawyer, one of two survivors of the Wallace House (December 14, 1926), was born in 1851. A lawyer by profession he was Solicitor of the Second Circuit in 1898, and resigned that position to volunteer for the War with Spain, commanding Co. L, First South Carolina Volunteer Infantry. At the close of that war. he was appointed by President McKinley a captain in the 38th United States Volunteers, and served with distinction with that command in the Philippine Islands for two years. Since then Captain Sawyer has been practicing his profession in Aiken.

†John C. Sheppard, the other survivor of the Wallace House, was born in 1850, and was admitted to the bar in 1871. When General W. H. Wallace, whose daughter Sheppard afterwards married, was elected Judge of the Seventh Circuit, in 1877, Sheppard was elected Speaker of the House to succeed him. He was re-elected in 1878 and again in 1880. In 1882, he was elected Lieutenant Governor, and when Hugh S. Thompson resigned as Governor, in 1886, towards the close of his second term to accept a position under Cleveland's administration, Sheppard became Governor, serving until December of that year. His last public service was that of State Senator from Edgefield County, 1898-1904, since which time he has been engaged in the practice of his profession in Edgefield.

INDEX